TEACH LIKE A PIRATE

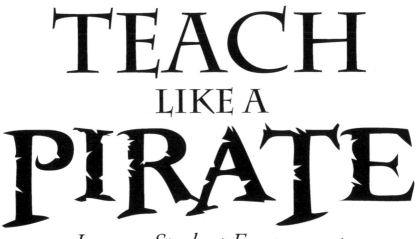

TEACH
LIKE A
PIRATE

Increase Student Engagement,
Boost Your Creativity, and
Transform Your Life as an Educator

DAVE BURGESS

DAVE BURGESS
Consulting, Inc.

SAN DIEGO, CALIFORNIA

Teach Like a PIRATE
© 2012 by Dave Burgess

This book is available at special discounts when purchased in quantity for use as premiums, promotions, fundraisers, or for educational use. For inquiries and details, contact the publisher at shelley@daveburgessconsulting.com.

Published by Dave Burgess Consulting, Inc.
San Diego, CA
www.daveburgessconsulting.com

Cover and Interior Design by Imagine! Studios, www.ArtsImagine.com
Cover Photos: iStockPhoto.com, Flickr.com
Editing and Production by My Writers' Connection

Library of Congress Control Number: 2012914927

ISBN: 978-0-9969896-2-6 (hardback)
ISBN: 978-0-9882176-0-7 (paperback)
ISBN: 978-0-9882176-1-4 (e-book)

Second Dave Burgess Consulting, Inc. Printing: January 2018

CONTENTS

ACKNOWLEDGMENTS

I would like to express my gratitude to the following people who were instrumental on my journey to create this book:

My wife, Shelley, for serving as a constant reminder that administrators and teachers are on the same team. You can read her amazing thoughts on educational leadership at **http://shelleyburgess.com**.

My children, Hayden and Ashlyn, for dealing with a distracted father while this was being written and for offering the opportunity to see school from a parent's perspective. I'd love for you to visit my daughter's blog at **http://ashlynburgess.com**.

My parents, Ann and Bill, for not only being great educators, but also for supporting me along the twists and turns that led to my current path.

My inner circle of educational linchpins: Dan McDowell, Reuben Hoffman, and John Berray.

My officemate, Jarrod Carman, for dealing with the ruckus and for the hundreds of office-walk conversations.

Billie Fogle, a special education teacher extraordinaire and my first period team-teacher for sixteen consecutive years and counting.

Bryan Ross, my colleague, friend, and Department Chair who encouraged an environment that honors individual expression in the classroom. I have made three significant career moves in my life; he has been instrumental in all three.

I built a publishing "dream team" to bring this book to fruition. Much thanks and gratitude to:

Erin Casey (**http://erin-casey.com**): My amazing editor who so beautifully polished my words while absolutely maintaining my voice.

Kristen and Joe Eckstein (**http://artsimagine.com**): They took my vision for the cover and interior design of this book and wonderfully brought it to life.

Penny Sansevieri (**http://amarketingexpert.com**): Her marketing advice and book launch campaign has helped me significantly expand the reach of my message.

INTRODUCTION

A PIRATE'S LIFE FOR ME

"Now and then we had a hope that if we lived and were good, God would permit us to be pirates."

MARK TWAIN, *LIFE ON THE MISSISSIPPI*

"Life's pretty good, and why wouldn't it be? I'm a pirate, after all."

JOHNNY DEPP

I've spent the past few years of my life traveling from conference to conference and school to school, dressed as a pirate.

I get some odd looks. But that's OK. I'm a teacher. Getting odd looks is part of the job.

I am on a crusade to spread the message of *Teach Like a PIRATE*—a system that can, like a treasure map, guide you to the reward of total transformation of your classroom and your life as an educator. In my book, that's worth a few odd looks.

Teach Like a PIRATE is part inspirational manifesto and part practical roadmap. My hope is that it will lead you to become more passionate, creative, and fulfilled in your role as a teacher. At the same time, my goal is to help you create an inviting, engaging, and most importantly, *empowering* classroom climate.

So why a pirate? After all, we don't want teachers who attack and rob ships at sea. Teaching like a pirate has nothing to do with the dictionary definition and everything to do with the spirit. Pirates are daring, adventurous, and willing to set forth into uncharted territories with no guarantee of success. They reject the status quo and refuse to conform to any society that stifles creativity and independence. They are entrepreneurs who take risks and are willing to travel to the ends of the earth for that which they value. Although fiercely independent, they travel with and embrace a diverse crew. If you're willing to live by the code, commit to the voyage, and pull your share of the load, then you're free to set sail. Pirates don't much care about public perception; they proudly fly their flags in defiance. And besides, everybody loves a pirate.

> *"The average man will bristle if you say his father is dishonest, but he'll brag a little if he discovers that his great-grandfather was a pirate."*
>
> BERN WILLIAMS

That description of the pirate's spirit sounds exactly like the kind of character we need more of in education. In these challenging and changing times, our students need leaders who are willing to venture forward without a clear map to explore new frontiers. We need mavericks and renegades who are willing to use unorthodox tactics to spark and kindle the flame of creativity and imagination in the minds of the young. We need entrepreneurial innovators who are capable of captaining the educational ship through waters that are rough and constantly changing. In short, we need pirates...we need you.

LAY OF THE LAND

Teach Like a PIRATE is divided into three parts:

PART I: TEACH LIKE A PIRATE

This is the heart of the PIRATE system and philosophy. It is divided into six chapters, one chapter for each letter of the word.

Passion—You know you're supposed to be passionate about your job as a teacher. This chapter explains *how* to feel passionate, even if the subject you're teaching isn't all that exciting to you.

Immersion—It's easy to shout directions from the safety of the sidelines, but the safe approach isn't the most effective one. To really engage your students you must be immersed in the moment. You'll learn in this chapter why your class needs your full attention.

Rapport—Getting to know your students on a personal level, showing them they are more than just a grade, and giving them a safe, fun environment sets the stage for learning. This chapter offers ideas on how to build rapport naturally and authentically so you can connect with your students.

Ask and Analyze—Coming up with creative ideas begins by asking the right questions. Making sure those ideas connect with your audience requires constant analysis and openness to feedback. This chapter will help you ask and analyze better so you can be a more creative and effective teacher.

Transformation—If you feel as though you're constantly hitting roadblocks with your students, maybe it's time to transform your expectations for what's possible in the classroom. This chapter explains how to reframe your subject—for yourself and your students—so you can break down those barriers.

Enthusiasm—Above all, enthusiasm is the most powerful tool in the classroom. This chapter explains why you must use it freely. You'll also learn how to ramp up your enthusiasm so your last class of the day receives the same high-impact lesson as your first class.

PART II: CRAFTING ENGAGING LESSONS

Are you tired of trying to talk over students who seem bent on ignoring you? This section will help you engage them and magnetically pull them into your lesson. In this crash course on designing presentations you'll find captivating hooks you can add to your content, as well as brainstorming questions to help you generate unbelievably engaging ideas for your lessons and skyrocket your creativity. The questions will spur you to think outside the box, and the applications give you some immediate and practical experience for implementing the creative process.

PART III: BUILDING A BETTER PIRATE

Before you set sail, you'll want to read these final instructions. In this section you'll find the reassurance and guidance needed to ensure that you reach your final destination and receive a treasure worthy of the voyage.

Welcome aboard!

TEACH LIKE
A PIRATE!

PASSION

"Only passions, great passions, can elevate the soul to great things."

DENIS DIDEROT

A huge secret lies deep in the heart of teachers all over the world. I know, because I am a teacher. You don't want to talk about it or admit it because you're fearful of the judgment of your peers. You see, you believe you are the only one who holds this seemingly terrible, ugly secret. It's like when Betty Friedan, in *The Feminine Mystique*, wrote that women all over the nation were lying in bed, staring at the ceiling and asking themselves, "Is this all?" They didn't want to discuss their feelings of emptiness and dissatisfaction with their peers because they thought they were alone and would face scorn and shame. Well, I'm hoping to be the Betty Friedan for you and I'm hoping this book will forever free you of this deep, dark secret that burdens your soul.

Here is the secret: *We are not passionate about* everything *we teach.* It's OK! Let the freedom wash over you. Now that the secret's out in the open, let's talk about it.

We know we are supposed to be passionate about teaching. That's why we feel guilty when that passion simply isn't there. We go to seminars and conferences where speakers explain why, as teachers, we must bring passion into our work. From the stage, we hear: "If you can't bring passion into your work then, by God, find new work!" It sounds great! We remember why we became teachers in the first place. We really *want* to help our students grow and succeed. For a moment, the enthusiastic messages get us excited and pumped up. But then the speakers leave the stage and we are left cold because they never explain *how* to find and maintain passion for teaching.

You know there are days when you look at the content standard and realize it's going to be tough to get yourself fired up. What do you do on those days? How can you consistently bring passion into your work as an educator even on the days you're teaching material you find boring or uninteresting?

I should, perhaps, mention there are rare exceptions…teachers who find everything about the subject they teach exciting. I call them freaks. I have one of them in my history department. He eats, sleeps, breathes, and "dresses" history on a daily basis. His house is like a museum. He is a reenactor in his spare time and has been an extra in numerous historical documentaries and movies. He, and people like him, don't need this section of the book. Good for them. The rest of us must intentionally find ways to bring passion to our work every day.

To solve this problem, I break passion into three distinct categories: Content Passion, Professional Passion, and Personal Passion. By consciously focusing on identifying, developing, and using all three of these categories, it is absolutely possible to become a powerfully passionate teacher every day of the school year. Take some time to answer the questions listed for each of these categories. To most effectively use this section, I recommend actually writing your answers down so you can refer to them later. At the very least *please* take the time to mentally complete the exercise before moving on.

CONTENT PASSION

Within your subject matter, what are you passionate about teaching? *In other words, of all of the topics and standards you teach as part of your curriculum, which are the ones you most enjoy?*

I am most passionate about teaching the Civil Rights Movement. I love everything about it, and within that unit there are even areas I am more passionate about than others. For example, I especially love to teach the edgier side of the movement. I don't need any extra help getting fired up when teaching about Malcolm X or the Black Panther Party. I don't have to work very hard to energize the room when discussing the ideas of Malcolm X. I enjoy meeting that "energy" head-on to try to open the minds of my students. I also love to teach about the resistance to slavery. And the counterculture of the sixties…no problem! My students love hearing the music from that time period that I use to help deliver the content.

On the other hand, I am *not* passionate about railroads! I understand their historical significance, but I don't stay up at night in anticipation of teaching about them. I'm also not real excited about the Industrial Revolution. I don't get too fired up about military history. So what can you and I do on the days where the subject matter doesn't fall into our content passion? That is where professional passion and personal passion come in.

PROFESSIONAL PASSION

Within your profession, but not specific to your subject matter, what are you passionate about? *What is it about being an educator that drives you? What ignites a fire inside you?*

I'll give you a hint on this one: Your answer probably consists of the reasons you became a teacher. Too often, as we manage the day-to-day stresses of the job, we fail to reconnect with the reasons we felt called to this sacred and invaluable profession in the first place. This is the all-important "life-changing" category and I invite you take the time to consider and write down your response.

My professional passion sounds like this: I'm passionate about creating lifelong learners. I'm passionate about increasing the self-esteem and self-confidence of my students. I'm passionate about having students leave my class with a larger vision of what is possible for their lives. I enjoy helping students who are apathetic about school get excited about coming to school, even if it is just because of my class. I love developing the creative and innovative spirit of my students. I am passionate about not letting them fall victim to the horrific educational trends that would have us turn children into test-taking automatons who are able to spit out facts and trivia but are unable to speak about anything of significance or meaning. I want to model and inspire a spirit of entrepreneurship and drive for constant self-improvement in all areas of life. I am also passionate about developing engaging presentations for my material.

Frankly, I could fill this book with examples of my professional passion because it is the real reason I became a teacher. Few people go into teaching because of their love for a particular subject. Not many English teachers chose their careers based on an undying passion to teach the effective and correct use of the comma. Math teachers rarely have an unnatural love of pi. I certainly was not drawn to the profession in order to teach railroads. Chances are you, like me, are a teacher because of your professional passion.

Here is the key: On all of those days when you don't have passion for your content, you must consciously make the decision to focus on your professional passion. This intentionality doesn't come naturally, at least not at first. That's why it is crucial to make the commitment to change your perspective and consistently focus on your professional passion. I constantly strive to include my professional passion in every lesson I teach with what I call life-changing lessons (LCLs). LCLs provide me the opportunity to attempt to transform the lives of my students regardless of my particular content standard for the day.

Incorporating an LCL, my true passion in education, also allows me to consistently "bring it." This focus gives me the juice to light up a classroom no matter what topic I might be teaching that day. For example, when I'm teaching about Malcolm X, there's a certain amount of factual, historical information I must deliver to my students. But I also have a hidden and larger agenda. I use Malcolm's life story to show my students the unbelievably incredible ability human beings have to transform their lives. Here was a man whose father was killed, most likely murdered, his mother placed in an institution, and he was raised in the foster care system. He dropped out of school after having his dreams and ambitions crushed by, of all people, a teacher. He eventually got involved with the wrong crowd, was arrested and convicted for breaking and entering, weapons charges, and burglary. While serving a ten-year jail sentence, he completely transformed his life through the power of self-education. He read book after book, took correspondence courses and became a highly educated man. He joined the Nation of Islam, changed his name and eventually became a Muslim minister and the national spokesperson for the Nation. After becoming disillusioned with the Nation of Islam's leader, taking a trip to Mecca and many other places overseas, he broke away from the organization and transformed his life and message yet again. He disavowed some of his earlier rhetoric and began delivering a new and powerful message that was more inclusive yet maintained his hardline ideology of self-determination and Black Nationalism. Just as he was refining this message and preparing to lead his new organization, he was gunned down while delivering a speech at the Audubon Ballroom. He was thirty-nine years old.

It's difficult to get to a much lower spot in life than having your father murdered, your mom in a mental institution, dropping out of school, and sitting in prison as a convicted felon. Yet Malcolm chose to rise above those huge, seemingly insurmountable obstacles and became an inspirational leader to thousands. I use Malcolm's story to show my students that no matter where they start in life, or how low they fall, they can still, through the power of self-education and their own efforts, rise to greatness.

A lesson on Abraham Lincoln becomes a lesson on persistence and overcoming adversity. The story of Rosa Parks shows that a single, ordinary person with strong convictions, and the courage to act on those convictions, can transform history. A D-Day lesson is an opportunity to teach appreciation and gratitude for the sacrifices made by previous generations to secure the liberties that we often take for granted today. Every lesson can include an LCL.

Professional passion can help fill the gaps you might have in content passion in other ways, as well. For example, I mentioned that I am not passionate about railroads. Fortunately for my students, I am passionate about developing engaging presentations for my material. So, although I might not be jazzed about the subject, I can absolutely be inspired and fully engaged in my attempt to present the topic in an entertaining way. I can be passionate about providing an opportunity for my students to develop and exercise their creative talents and abilities. I can be passionate about creating the atmosphere and social dynamic necessary to build rapport and a psychologically safe environment.

Professional passion is an absolute treasure chest filled with everything we need to steadfastly refuse to enter the classroom with anything less than a burning hot passion for the awesome job and responsibility that lies before us. Tap into it and feel the power surge through your soul!

PERSONAL PASSION

Completely outside of your profession, what are you passionate about?

I'm passionate about magic. I'm passionate about sports, especially basketball and coaching. I'm passionate about my family. I'm passionate about entrepreneurship, marketing, and self-improvement.

To keep your passion for teaching alive, find as many ways as possible to incorporate your personal passions into your work. Whenever I can use magic to demonstrate a point, I absolutely do it. Not only does that help me create a more engaging and therefore memorable lesson, it also helps increase my sense of fulfillment and fun as an educator.

Almost every personal passion can be incorporated into the classroom. For example, are you passionate about art and creativity? Develop lessons that showcase your passion and allow your students to not only experience your unique strengths, skills, and imagination, but also begin to develop their own. If you are passionate about playing the guitar, bring it in and play. I know teachers who have an incredible interest in cutting-edge technology. They find ways to incorporate their tech skills into their lessons. Bringing your personal passion to the classroom empowers you to create a more powerful lesson because you are teaching from an area of strength. And bonus: it also allows your students to see how *their* unique skill sets and passions can be vital, invaluable, and applicable for their future.

> *"Individuality of expression is the beginning and end of all art."*
> JOHANN WOLFGANG VON GOETHE

If you're having difficulty figuring out how your personal passion can be used in the classroom, don't stress out. You may just need a little help in the art of creative brainstorming. Later portions of this book focus specifically on skyrocketing your creativity and mastering the brainstorming process. It's also important to realize that unlike professional passion, personal passion isn't likely to be something that can or should be included in your lesson plans on a daily basis. Rather, it is more like a bonus category that offers you opportunities to really ramp up your love of teaching when it works out.

By tapping into all three categories of passion—and especially consciously dedicating yourself to an increased daily focus on professional passion—you will become an unstoppable "passion monster" in the classroom. Your increased passion will sustain you through those long stretches of the year that inevitably arrive and attempt to drag you down. Teaching is a job filled with frustrations, trials, and tests of your patience. Use your passion to soar over obstacles instead of crashing into them and burning out.

Your passion will also help you become absolutely relentless in the pursuit of excellence. With a focus on professional passion, teaching is no longer about relaying the content standard…it's about transforming lives. It's about killing apathy. It's about helping the next generation fulfill their potential and become successful human beings. It's no longer about memorizing facts; it's about inspiring greatness.

When you're passion-filled, you also become more personally fulfilled as an educator. It's fun and exciting to share what is uniquely "you." Doing so makes your presentations and personal charisma almost magnetic in nature. Being in the presence of people who are engaged in fulfilling their major life purpose is almost hypnotic. There is a certain "juice," an electricity, that emanates from those who truly love what they are doing or discussing. Others may have no particular interest in the subject at hand, but they are magically drawn to a person because of the sheer power that permeates the presentation. Passion is like an intoxicating drug but without the dangers and side effects. Use it as much as you want. Once you get a taste of it, you'll always want to come back for more.

BIRDS, SNAKES, AND THE ART OF TEACHING

Not long ago, I was with my two kids and two dogs at a small pond in a Tierrasanta canyon when we came across a man walking his dogs and wearing binoculars around his neck. As we were sharing small talk, he suddenly stopped and whipped the binoculars up to his face and excitingly pointed out a hawk perched on top of a nearby tree. He told us the type of hawk it was, its hunting behavior, and how its feathers were specially designed for the type of flight maneuvers it needed.

I was fascinated.

Now please understand, I couldn't care less about hawks, and I'm about as far from an outdoorsman as you will ever find. My idea of camping is a hotel room or a cruise ship cabin. So why was I drawn in by this man's story? How did he hold my attention for thirty minutes as he discussed the entire ecosystem surrounding the pond and gave an impassioned argument for not killing rattlesnakes?

The answer is simple. This man was one hundred percent passionate about his subject. When you interact with someone who is fully engaged and filled with passion, it can be an overwhelming and unforgettable experience. There is no faking it...you can't "Meg Ryan" that type of passion! Enthusiasm, yes...passion, no.

There is a type of vibration that seems to emanate from people who are fulfilling their definite major purpose in life, and it is contagious. I still don't particularly care about the ten types of birds he told me to watch for, but I would listen to him talk about them any day of the week. My kids talked about the man the entire way home.

People are drawn in and love to be around those who are passionate about their lives.

It doesn't matter what subject you teach. You can become totally engaging to your audience if they can feel your passion and love for what you are doing. You will draw students in as if by some magnetic force. Passion is all about being on fire in front of your class. I'm fond of the quote, "Light yourself on fire with enthusiasm and people will come from miles around just to watch you burn!"

This is yet another reason a "cookie cutter" approach to teaching will never be the most effective. What gets me fired up and passionate in the classroom, and therefore more effective, might not be the answer for my colleague down the hall. Resist any movement that attempts to clone teachers and lessons and instead rejoice in the fact that it is your individuality and uniqueness that will always lead you to become the most effective teacher that you can be.

Light yourself on fire with passion...and don't worry if it's not a controlled burn.

IMMERSION

"Do whatever you do intensely."
ROBERT HENRI

You're about learn the #1, *top secret* way to become a *dramatically better lover!*

I have your attention now, don't I?

Right now, the people reading this can be split into two groups… men and women. The men are thinking, "I definitely don't need this section." The women are thinking, "I sure hope the men are paying attention to this section!" (I should mention that my wife is probably thinking, "What the heck is he doing thinking he can teach this subject?")

In the famous science-fiction book, *Stranger in a Strange Land* by Robert Heinlein, there is a female character who has had an "encounter" with a man by the name of Mike. It was a completely overwhelming experience; one she has a great deal of difficulty putting into words. When asked about it by another person, she feels frustrated at her inability to accurately describe her feelings. Finally, she says, "When Mike's kissing you, he isn't doing anything else. You're his whole universe." In other words, the whole rest of the world disappeared and every single cell, fiber, muscle, and thought was fully immersed in the moment.

The secret to becoming a better lover—and a better teacher—is total *immersion*. Your ability to completely give yourself up to the moment and fully "be" with your students is an awesome and unmistakably powerful technique. I would love for one of my students to be talking with a peer about what it is like to be in my class on a daily basis and for that student to say, "When he's teaching you, he isn't doing anything else!" Students can feel it when you are truly present.

As easy as it is to sense immersion, students can also immediately sense when we aren't all there. We all know when we are dealing with people who are distracted or are in some way dividing their attention. Whether it is a cashier, your doctor, a friend, or anyone else, a lack of full engagement can be annoying. It's incredibly frustrating to interact with a person who is not immersed and fully invested in that interaction. A lack of immersion in the present sends a clear, although unspoken, message that this moment is somehow less important and not significant enough to be worth undivided attention.

Here's one way to illustrate immersion. If you are out on the pool deck and someone asks you to focus on the swimming pool, what does that mean? Would you go stand at the side and stare at it? Would you climb into the lifeguard tower and watch from above? Focus is, after all, supposed to be a powerful and effective strategy. Now compare the concept of focus with the next scenario that defines immersion. You're on the pool deck and someone tells you to immerse yourself in the swimming pool. What would this look like? What is implied when someone asks you to immerse yourself in a pool? You're wet! You're in the water! You're either swimming or you're drowning. It is a qualitatively different experience.

I can walk by the open door of a classroom and tell you after a couple of minutes whether the teacher is a lifeguard or a swimmer. A lifeguard sits above the action and supervises the pool deck. Although he or she is focused, there is a distinct sense of separateness both physically and mentally. In contrast, a swimmer is out participating and an integral part of the action.

Last summer, my son Hayden took swim lessons at the local YMCA two days a week. On Tuesdays, he had a male coach who stood at the side of the pool and gave instructions as he returned after each lap. On Thursdays, he had a female instructor who was *in* the pool with Hayden. She physically lifted his arms and showed him the proper strokes. She would take his chin and move his head to the side to demonstrate how far out of the water he should come to take a breath. He learned more on one or two Thursdays than he did on all of the Tuesdays put together.

It's far more powerful to "swim" with your students. They need the benefit of your complete immersion. Now, it is important to point out that my son was learning the strokes for the first time as opposed to practicing and perfecting strokes that he had already learned. To be clear, I'm not suggesting that a competitive swim coach needs to be in the water with his athletes. I'm suggesting that when delivering first instruction, especially to struggling learners, you need to leave the comfort of the lounge chair or lifeguard tower and jump into the water with your students.

Immersion is felt by students in ways we don't even realize. I missed a couple days of school recently and had my substitute teacher show a video. Upon return, several students complained that it just wasn't the same watching with the sub. I said, "What do you mean? The whole period was going to be spent watching the video whether I was here or not." To which one of my students replied, "Yeah, but you always pause the video to tell us cool things and build up anticipation for what's coming. You make little comments the whole time. We like that you watch and react to the video with us. It's just different when you're here." That eye-opening conversation offered dramatic proof of the significant difference personal power, attitude, and full presence of the instructor has on the learning environment. An instructor who is fully immersed in the moment has a special type of intensity that resonates with great power in the classroom, regardless of the activity.

The sun is a powerful source of heat, yet the Earth doesn't burst into flames each day at noon. However, if you concentrate the sun's rays through a magnifying glass and direct the narrow beam towards something flammable you can start a fire. That is the difference between dissipated energy and energy that has been captured, concentrated and directed into a powerful laser-like focus. Immersion works the same way in the classroom and will allow you to morph lukewarm lessons into supernovas that set the classroom on fire.

DON'T MISS THE MOMENT

I had a major reminder of one of my seminar principles over Thanksgiving week. I was home with my two children every day all week while my wife was working. Normally, this would be fine, but I also had several things I was working on...like sitting at the computer and brainstorming blog ideas. As my children competed for my divided attention, I felt the beginnings of frustration creeping in (OK, OK, more than the beginnings!). Right before I snapped, it hit me; sometimes I need to take my own damn seminar. I teach this stuff! I was not following the principle of "immersion." Divided attention is ineffective and creates a major loss of personal power. I set my work aside and made the firm decision to just "be" with my kids. Immersion in that moment meant being *fully* present, going with the flow, and surrendering my need to be in control all the time.

How did it end up? We had an incredible day exploring the canyons of Tierrasanta and going wherever they wanted. As we chatted along the way, I witnessed the innate creativity children can show when not over-scheduled and "structured" to death. By the way, by personally letting go, I also freed my mind to come up with blog topics naturally. I got more ideas and clarity by taking a walk than I ever would have by staring at a computer screen. Sometimes we need to give our brain the vision and then let our conscious mind get out of the way and let the unconscious do its thing.

The practice of immersion and letting yourself fully experience the moment applies to the classroom in more ways than I can possibly mention. I'm a firm believer in having structure and definite plans for the direction of lessons, but sometimes things happen that demand a change in direction and a "letting go" of the plan. The teachable moment is called that because if you wait *it will be gone!* It's OK to surrender your structure in the pursuit of something far more valuable in the moment.

"But wait...the state test is coming up soon. Surely my students will never recover and get back on pace."

Well, here's what I say: At some point in your career you have to decide if you care more about teaching to tests or teaching kids. My decision was made a long time ago. I teach kids. Don't let the current overemphasis on standardized test scores lead to the loss of the teachable moment. Having the right structure and using your time in the classroom effectively allows you the flexibility to let "the moment" happen without any sense of guilt. Sometimes we need to just "be" with our students and take the figurative walk through the canyons with them.

RAPPORT

*"One hundred victories in one hundred battles
is not the most skillful. Subduing the other's
military without battle is the most skillful."*

SUN TZU

The quote above from Sun Tzu's *The Art of War* is one of the greatest behavior management quotes in history. Ultimately, we don't want to develop techniques to win behavior management battles, we want to develop techniques that allow us to *avoid the battles altogether.*

I know for a fact I have many students who are a living nightmare for the other teachers on their schedule, but present me with very little difficulty. How is this possible? It certainly isn't that I am more knowledgeable in my subject matter. It rarely has to do with me having a higher level of compassion or being more caring than my colleagues. Nor do I believe those students' inconsistent behavior has anything to do with me having greater skill in behavior management.

So what compels these "trouble makers" to behave in my class? First and foremost, I believe it's because they are engaged. It is my opinion and experience that an engaged student is rarely a behavior problem. Misbehavior usually indicates boredom, overwhelm, or lack of connection to the material being covered. The entire second half of this book offers an in-depth study on transforming your lessons into highly engaging presentations that draw in and hold your students' interest like a magnet. But engagement is only one piece of the behavior puzzle. Equally important to your success in avoiding battles with students is your ability to develop deep levels of rapport.

You can't effectively develop engaging presentations unless you spend the necessary time and effort to find out what they already find engaging. Many of the strategies I will describe later are universal in nature and designed to work for all audiences. They play off of basic human nature and can be safely and effectively used across the board. However, one of the big secrets and shortcuts to engagement is to spend less time trying to get students interested in what you are presenting and more time making connections between what you are presenting and what they are *already* interested in.

I start building rapport on the very first day of school with my Play-Doh lesson. I continue to try to learn as much as I can about my students as the year goes on. What are their hobbies? What sports do they play? What types of music do they listen to? What movies do they like? Which TV shows do they love to watch? If you're paying attention to what excites them, you can connect with them almost instantly. Some of my killer hooks for lessons have come directly from picking up on conversations I overhear between students.

You can also ask students to try to find connections between your content and pop culture. Many times, students bring to my attention the relationship a currently popular song or movie has to what we are studying. You should do everything you can to encourage your students to draw these types of connections.

Similarly, try reading the paper and watching the news with your class in mind. Develop the habit of combing current events from the perspective of searching for hooks and connections to your material.

You will be astonished at the gold mine that surrounds you. This habit offers the added benefit of consistently keeping your lessons fresh and more interesting for you, as well.

An additional key to developing rapport is spending informal time with your students. Use the minutes between classes, before and after school, and occasionally at lunch and break to connect with them. For example, several clubs use my room at lunchtime. I believe being available to kids says a lot to them about whether or not you are interested in them beyond your particular class. Try to interact with them during passing periods and stop and chat or say "hi" as you pass on campus during the day. As often as you can, attend extra-curricular activities your students are involved in. Building rapport is all about interacting with your students as fellow human beings, not just as subordinates. Kids can tell the difference between teachers who only seem to care about them when they are sitting in the classroom, and those who see past the "student" to the unique person who resides inside.

> *"I have yet to find a man, however exalted his station, who did not do better work and put forth greater effort under a spirit of approval than under a spirit of criticism."*
>
> CHARLES SCHWAB

Rapport is also incredibly important because it helps create buy-in. When I discuss some of the things my students do, I know many teachers think to themselves, "There's no way my kids would do that." They might be right! My kids probably wouldn't do it on the first day of school. They don't know or trust me yet. But by working to create a safe and supportive environment where students feel valued, I earn their trust. You can, too.

I actively encourage teachers to develop a classroom climate where students *feel like* doing the outrageous; where the out of the ordinary and sometimes silly are the norm. How do I foster this environment?

> *"I learned that when I made people laugh, they liked me. This is a lesson I'll never forget."*
>
> ART BUCHWALD

First, I model the behavior I want from my student. I am perfectly comfortable in my own skin and am willing to "let my hair down" in the classroom. An uptight and stiff teacher leads to an uptight and stiff class. Get playful! Allow for friendly banter. Put a premium on making your class fun and entertaining right from the start.

MY FIRST THREE DAYS

I have spent quite a bit of time thinking about and designing my first three days of school. You probably have your routine, and that's fine. My goal in describing my first three days isn't to get you to implement them instead of what you already do. I'm more concerned with demonstrating the thinking behind what I do so you can evaluate which if any of these ideas will work for you. As with the rest of this book, this is not an all or nothing situation; you may want to incorporate only a few of these ideas into what you already do. On the other hand, maybe you'll decide you want to completely revamp your opening days. Either way, I hope these thoughts are helpful.

Nothing is more important to me than creating the proper atmosphere right from the start. No content standard matters to me until I have established the safe, supportive, and positive classroom environment I need to successfully teach my students. Any time I spend on the front end of the year to establish this environment is *not* time wasted. In fact, I know it will pay dividends a hundred times over before the end of the year.

DAY ONE

The first thing students see when they approach my door is a sign like you might see outside of a theme park ride, a haunted house, or some extreme sport activity. On it is my name and room number and the words:

"YOU'VE HEARD THE STORIES...

ARE YOU READY FOR THE EXPERIENCE?!!"

Before my new students even enter my room, they are hit with a rather unusual and intriguing message that plays off the fact that many legendary, often exaggerated, stories circulate around the campus community about what happens in my room. Even if a student has never heard one of these stories, the sign's message creates an interesting sense of anticipation. They immediately wonder, *What in the world is this class all about?*

As they enter the room, the first thing students notice is the positive, upbeat energy created by the music playing. I always use music during my passing periods to create an immediate break from the hustle, bustle, and drama of the hallways. It is an audible reminder that they are entering a different world...my world.

Next, their eyes will focus on the desks. Every desk has a paper plate with a can of Play-Doh on it. Across the board, written in giant letters, are the words, "Do NOT Open the Play-Doh!" Already, I am trying to break their pre-conceived notions about what to expect in a typical classroom. My goal is to stand out, to be different from their other classes. High school kids are not used to playing with Play-Doh, and it is certainly a pattern interrupt that breaks the monotony of the typical first day spent reading the class syllabus and reciting classroom rules and procedures. In my opinion, it is far more important to create a unique experience for them on the first day than it is to be sure they know how many bathroom passes they will have each semester and when it is OK to use the pencil sharpener!

I take care of all necessary first day administrative tasks such as taking attendance and checking their schedules to be sure they are in the right place before I "officially" greet them. Once I start, I don't want there to be any transitions that will slow me down and impede the flow of the lesson. Eliminating and smoothing out transitions is a key element to maintaining engagement and one I will discuss further in the section on hooks.

With the boring stuff out of the way, I proceed to give them what I refer to as "Good Morning Training." This is extremely tough to describe in writing and really must be experienced to fully understand. Basically, I stand behind my rolling table in the front of the room and draw all attention to myself as I go through a bizarre process of squaring up the papers in front of me, adjusting the angle of the table, and awkwardly straightening myself up to address the class. If done correctly, there should be a combination of a few giggles and many wondering what the heck is going on. I then look up and say, "Good Morning" in a loud, firm voice. I wait in silence until I hear a smattering of good mornings and then storm through the class ranting that their response is totally unacceptable and will not be tolerated. "Not one single time will I accept that from you! When I say 'good morning' to you, you say 'good morning' to me. Not only that, but however I say good morning to you is how you say good morning to me! If I say 'Good Morning!' (said with strange accent)…you say 'Good Morning!' (said with exact same accent). Let's try this again, this is your first test of the year and yes…I am grading!" I then return to the front, face the class, and whisper my greeting. They should respond in kind and then I say, "Welcome to class, thank you for coming. I'm Dave Burgess and I'll be your host on this Learning Extravaganza!!"

At this point, I am off and running. Looking out at my class, I see students looking like they have been hit by a hurricane of energy and a burst of fire. Under their breath students say things like:

"This is going to be awesome."

"My friend said that this guy is crazy."

"This guy is totally on drugs."

What you don't hear is students saying, "This looks like it is going to be a boring class." I want them to immediately realize they have entered a space unlike any other they have ever experienced.

Next, I give them a handout titled:

WELCOME TO THE WORLD FAMOUS LEARNING EXTRAVAGANZA!

HOSTED BY: DAVE BURGESS

NOW PLAYING IN SS-9

Notice the positioning that is used in that title. It doesn't say "U.S. History/Geo 1C." It says "World Famous Learning Extravaganza." It is "hosted" by me, not taught. And it is "playing in SS-9" as if they have entered a show.

It is as close to a set of rules and procedures as I will ever give them. I fly through it in a humorous fashion, but really zero in on one item. I let them know this class will be completely different than anything they have ever attended. To succeed they must suspend their pre-conceived notions about what is allowed in a classroom and get into the spirit of helping to create an outrageously fun and entertaining experience. I openly tell them I believe this will be their favorite class of all time and one that they will remember forever… but that it only works if we agree to follow one rule:

THIS IS A NO-MEANNESS ZONE!!

I let them know I will tolerate unbelievable levels of banter, playfulness, and seemingly outrageous behavior for a classroom, but I will *never* tolerate meanness. All of the fun will come grinding to a stop if somebody is being mean to another student or doing something that hurts another's feelings. You just can't teach with my style of openness without emphasizing this rule. It is critical for creating the safe and supportive kind of environment in which creativity, learning, and fun can coexist and flourish. As part of this rule, I also tell them they should feel free to let me know if I am making them feel uncomfortable by drawing unwanted attention to them through my banter and teasing. I want my students to feel perfectly at ease approaching me about any issue that is occurring in class. Creating a place of safety is a prerequisite for the successful implementation of my teaching style.

Once everyone knows the rules, I tell students to take the next ten minutes to create something with their dough that is in some way representative of themselves. They can have complete creative license to make anything they want as long as it is classroom appropriate. I explain that I will show the class their creation, ask a question or two about it, and have them tell us their name. They will not have to come to the front of the room and the whole process will take thirty seconds or less. That simple explanation of what to expect helps lower the stress some students feel about speaking in the front of the class.

When they begin to work on their artistic creation, I get a chance to do something important but rare on the first day of school. I get to walk around and informally interact with my students. I help them brainstorm ideas for what to create if they are stuck (again lowering stress levels), and I get a chance to begin to learn about my students by asking them questions about their creations. This information can later be used to help to create hooks for my material that are highly effective because they incorporate subjects in which they are already involved and engaged.

When the time is up, I make my way quickly up and down the rows talking to each student and having them introduce themselves. As I ask questions about what they created, I keep it quick, light-hearted, and filled with humorous banter. I "rescue" any student who is struggling to find something to say so that everyone leaves class feeling like they have been successful.

Throughout the class period I make a major point of going back over the names multiple times. In fact, I offer a prize to any student who can tell me the name of every student in class at the end of the activity. I will allow them to do this at any point during my first week of school. I believe it is critical for students to at least know each other's names if we are trying to build an environment with a high level of rapport.

At the end of the class period, I thank the students for coming and then say something along the lines of, "You don't want to miss tomorrow. Something wild and crazy is going to happen at the beginning of class. You can either be here and see it, or just have to hear stories about it when you come back." You better believe that makes them curious enough to *want* to come to class the next day.

I want to pause and make a comment here about building rapport—with the students, and among the students. Several years ago, I learned the hard way that many students do not even know who is sitting in class with them. I asked three students to help me pass back papers during the last few minutes of a class period. When the bell rang they each brought me back a stack of papers. I was horrified to discover they did not return the papers, not because they ran out of time, but because they did not know who the people were. Now understand, this was about halfway through the school year. Here I was, traveling around the country speaking to audiences about subjects such as building rapport, and I had students who didn't even know the name of the kid sitting behind them. Since that moment, I have it made it a point to emphasize names as part of what I do during the first three days. Making it into a contest helps get some buy-in.

DAY TWO

Day two begins with my opening ritual that was a part of their "Good Morning Training" from the first day. I then turn off the lights, return to the front of the room, and transform myself into an airplane. I fly full-speed around the room twice with my arms outstretched and jet motor fully audible. As I am returning to the front to finish the second lap, I apparently trip, fling myself onto the floor, and roll a couple of times. As I straighten up to my knees, I act as if I am taking in breaths and dog-paddling in water. I alternate between putting my head down under the water with gurgling noises and then catching some breaths at the surface. I motion wildly and shout that I see a life raft…and then I "swim" on the floor towards it. I pull the cord, make the noise of it inflating, and then climb in. I start pulling imaginary people into the raft, struggling with each of them until I count and have ten survivors.

I then (careful with this one!) pass out for an awkwardly long period of time. Trust me on this, on the second day of school with a teacher passed out on the floor after crashing in a plane and swimming on the carpet, an awkwardly long period of time is very short! I come to, pretend to see land, and then hand paddle to it. I pull the raft up onto the beach and discover a deserted island.

After some by-play, I make helicopter sounds, wave it down, and then simulate the wind of its landing. I become the copter pilot stepping out and tell the survivors that I have never seen this island on any map, I was blown off course and am unsure that I will be able to locate it again. My copter can only accommodate five passengers, so five will come back to safety and five will have to survive on the island. It is up to the class to decide who will be saved and who will be left behind. They are to form collaborative groups of three or four students each and come to a consensus.

I provide them with a list of the ten characters who have survived the crash. Each of these characters is designed to cause a debate as to whether they should stay or go. For example, one is a botanist who is also the single mom of two young children. Some will want to keep her on the island for her knowledge of plants and others will want to return her to her children. Another example is a convicted murderer who is on parole. Some students won't want to give him one of the five seats home. Other students may not want to leave four people on the island with him. The whole idea is to create characters that will spark a debate and differences in opinion.

This exercise accomplishes two main goals. First, they are once again socked in the stomach with an outrageous and outside-the-box intro to the period that is not only bizarre, but highly entertaining. Secondly, I get the chance to discuss group dynamics, the collaborative process, and the procedures we use to get into groups, all in the context of a fun, engaging activity that does not have any particular right or wrong answers. The answer to who is rescued and who stays on the island doesn't matter; it is the process that is important. I emphasize that they must not only come to a consensus, but they must be able to justify their answers.

As the groups collaborate, I circulate through the room and monitor the process. I reinforce proper dynamics, the no-meanness rule, and encourage full participation. Once finished, each group reports their answers and responds to any questions I might have about their choices. It is always interesting to see how different the answers can be and how the justifications vary from group to group and from period to period. I track the responses on a chart on the board.

After two days, every student has introduced themselves to the whole class and has participated in a collaborative group. In addition, they have yet to see anything resembling an ordinary class experience.

They leave wondering what in the world is going to happen next. I'll tell you what is going to happen next, just the single most important day of the school year...Day Three!

DAY THREE

If I were to rank all of my one hundred eighty class days in order of importance, I would probably rank day three as the single most critical of the year. This is the day I explain the method to my madness and break down all possibilities of students falling into a self-fulfilling prophecy of failure. I teach many students who have struggled in school and failed many times before they arrive at my door. I know many of them are asking an unspoken question that is absolutely critical for me to be able to answer. I visualize them sitting in front of me and asking this silent question: "Why will I be successful in your class if I've never been successful before?" Until, and unless, I can answer that question, I don't believe I can effectively start my year.

Day three consists of a massive, high-energy, frenetic sales pitch designed to convince my students that my class is completely different from anything they have ever experienced in school. Most importantly, I work to sell them on the fact that they can, and absolutely will, be successful. Far too many of our students have been beaten up by school. They have been told they don't measure up. They have been made to believe their unique gifts and talents are not valued by the educational system because they are not reflected in test scores. They don't believe that school respects and honors their individuality but instead uses it against them as a tool to force conformity.

Every student in your class in those first few days of the semester is evaluating whether or not your room is an emotionally and psychologically safe environment. They're wondering if it is worth their time and effort to give school a real shot. After all, it's easier to not give your best and then blame failure on a lack of effort, than to be forced to realize you really don't have what it takes. At least you can save face with your peers when you fail if you don't try in the first place.

None of this is ever verbally expressed. However, if you teach the same clientele I do, you know this is what some of them are thinking. It is our job as teachers to address the unspoken thoughts rattling around in the minds of our students. The earlier we do it, the better.

My goal is to completely smash any idea my students might have about my class being more of the same for them. I will pull out all the stops to convince them it doesn't matter if they have failed before because my class is absolutely and completely different. My class has been specially designed for them to be successful. It is based on the latest brain research and incorporates incredible mnemonics designed to help them easily learn and retain more content in less time. I explain to them how the brain works and how a positive learning environment is critical for higher-order thinking to take place.

I talk to them about learning styles. I spend a great deal of time discussing Howard Gardner's theory of multiple intelligences. I give them compelling examples of how school systems have consistently neglected and undervalued many of these types of intelligences because they are not on "the test." I show how special gifts and talents, like artistic and musical creativity, should be equally valued in school. I talk to the athletes and dancers about kinesthetic intelligence. I give examples of how people with interpersonal intelligence might find themselves in trouble in school but have incredible opportunities for success in the "real world."

I do not have a casual, nonchalant attitude about this day. Make no mistake about it…I am *selling*! I believe great teaching incorporates many of the same skills and techniques used in successful salesmanship and marketing—and I use them all. By offering a powerfully compelling and engaging argument, I am attempting to fully persuade my students that they will be successful. I'm spinning the story to the best of my ability. But the difference between me and the PR masters who spin stories for the media is that I am convinced that what I'm selling is absolutely worthy of the effort. Marketers spend billions of dollars and untold hours trying to sell people products that don't even come close in significance to what I'm selling. I'm selling education…a life-altering product that can transform the human spirit and literally change the world one student at a time. Surely, such a product is worthy of any and all efforts, techniques, and methods required to successfully persuade.

At the very least, I want the most difficult and stubborn student in my class to leave with an open mind and say to themselves, "OK, maybe this guy is on to something. I'll give this a shot and see what happens." BOOM! I got him. That opening is all I need. Next comes the fun part: living up to my pitch and providing a course that knocks their socks off and rocks their world.

How do you do that? Just keep reading!

ASK AND ANALYZE

"Always the beautiful answer who asks
a more beautiful question."

E.E. CUMMINGS

"The important thing is not to stop questioning."

ALBERT EINSTEIN

"Questions are the laser of human consciousness."

ANTHONY ROBBINS

One of the most frequent questions I am asked is, "How can I become more creative when I'm designing my lessons?" More often, actually, it sounds something like this, "I love all of your examples, but how can I add those types of presentations to my lessons when I'm not as creative as you are?" Questions like that tell me I am speaking to yet another person who has fallen victim to what I call *the myth of the blinding flash of light*. Many people believe only two kinds of people exist in this world—those who are creative and those who are not. The people who believe this, of course, have usually already classified themselves into the latter category. They believe creative people simply walk around and are suddenly struck by creative ideas much like a bright flash of light. They are frustrated by the absence of that flash of light in their own lives. "If only I could get those same flashes of insight and creativity," they lament. "It's not fair!"

Maybe certain types of "genius" individuals, like Einstein, receive those flashes, but that's not how creativity happens for most people. For most of us, creative genius is developed through hard work, directed attention, and relentless engagement in the creative process.

What is this creative process? To a large extent, it is the process of consistently asking the right questions. I learned one of my most life-transforming concepts from motivational speaker and author, Anthony Robbins. The concept is the unbelievable importance and significance of questions. The types of questions we ask ourselves determine the types of answers that we receive. If you consistently ask questions that lead to creative and outside-the-box thinking, your mind will provide you with creative and outside-the-box answers. Asking the right questions is like tuning the radio to the correct frequency. Most people go through life listening to "creative static" because they have failed to properly tune their mind to the right station. In fact, most people don't even realize they have the ability to be creative, so they don't even bother to turn on the radio.

The quality of your questions determines the quality of your answers, and the type of question determines the type of ideas your brain will receive and conceive. A teacher approached me after attending one of my workshops and told me that he really liked my examples of how I take my classes outside of the room for multiple lessons. He went on to say that he couldn't think of any similar ideas for his classes. The question I asked him next revealed the reason he was stuck. I asked, "When you are designing your lessons, do you ask yourself, 'Is there a way I can get my class outside of the room for this lesson?' Or have you asked, 'Where is the best place on campus to deliver this lesson?'" His answer, of course, was no. How could he expect to find a creative way to get his class outside if he never asks the question? He was waiting for the blinding flash of light. Are you?

If you ask yourself, "Where is the best place on campus to deliver this lesson?" You might find that the answer is not your room. You'll never know if you don't ask. We can tweak and refine the questions to make them even better. For example, "How can I get my class outside for this lesson?" is better than "Is there a way…" because the latter allows for the mind to take the easy way out and just say "No." Even better might be to ask, "How many different ways can I find to get my class outside for this lesson?" Now the question naturally leads towards receiving multiple solutions rather than being satisfied with one. The ability to manipulate questions to make them even more effective is crucial to success in the creative process.

Another teacher approached me after a workshop, frustrated with his inability to think of any creative "board message" ideas. I put the same question to him, "Have you ever asked yourself, 'What could I write on my board for this lesson that would spark a conversation or create a buzz even before the bell rings?'" You can guess his answer. Creative ideas don't come out of the blue; they come from engaging in the creative process. That critical process starts when you ask the right types of questions and then actively seek the answers.

What we experience in our life is a direct result of our focus. Here's a real-life experience that drives home this truth. See if you can relate. Several years ago, my family entered the minivan stage. With two young children, we needed a more spacious form of transportation; my wife said we needed to think about getting a minivan. I knew absolutely nothing about minivans. I had never driven one, and didn't even know any of the brand names. To my recollection, I had never even ridden in one. Up to that point, the amount of time I had spent thinking about minivans was exactly zero. After a little online research, we visited the Honda dealership to test drive an Odyssey. I can honestly say I had no idea what an Odyssey was until that day. Afterwards, we crossed the street to test drive a Sienna at the Toyota dealership. I preferred the Odyssey, so we went back to the Honda dealership and bought a brand new, silver Odyssey.

On that day, at that moment, something absolutely amazing happened. Thousands and thousands of people got Odysseys at the exact same time as me. I saw them everywhere! On the way home I passed Odyssey after Odyssey. A Honda Odyssey merged into traffic in front of me. I pulled up to a stoplight right behind an Odyssey. I looked in the rearview mirror and there was one behind me, as well. At the supermarket, I parked between two Honda Odysseys. Three times since my purchase, I have actually opened the door to someone else's Honda Odyssey. Have you ever experienced that awkward moment when you realize it's someone else's stuff in the car you just opened the door to? I have, and the only thing you can do is quickly close the door, walk away, and hope no one saw you trying to get into a stranger's car.

I know you know the answer to this question but I'm going to ask it anyway: Did everybody get a Honda Odyssey the same day I did? No? Are you trying to tell me that all those Odysseys were there the whole time? Yes? Then why didn't I see them?

The answer reveals something incredible about the human mind. We are hit with so much information and stimuli that our brain cannot hope to process it all. We simply can't make sense of the world without a mental filter. The brain learns to attend to stimuli that it believes are important to you and to delete, or filter out, everything else. Until we needed a minivan, Odysseys weren't important to me. I never focused on them, or even gave them a second thought, so they just registered to my brain as "car" in the generic. Once I had an Odyssey and it was part of my life, my brain automatically attended to them and registered them as something special and different from just any car.

I'm sure you have had a similar experience. No sooner do you get involved or interested in a new subject than, out of nowhere, you see an article about it, a news report on it, and overhear other people discussing it in conversation. Your Reticular Activating System (RAS), the same neurological system that filters out unnecessary stimuli, begins to search for and point out thoughts, images, words, people, and places you never noticed before. Suddenly, your mental radio—your RAS—picks up an all new frequency, and it's tuned into your subject of interest.

The same principle holds true for creative ideas. Just like the Odysseys, creative ideas are all around us all of the time. Creative inspiration is constantly at our disposal, but we will never see it unless we actively and consistently attempt to create. By asking the right questions, you tune your RAS into your need for creative inspiration and solutions. Suddenly, clarity and creativity seem inescapable.

On a recent trip to Mobile, Alabama, I witnessed the power of this neurological phenomenon in action. I was presenting three days of workshops for the social studies teachers in the Mobile County School System. My friend Nate Smith, the Social Studies Coordinator, booked the event at the beautiful Museum of Mobile. After attending the day-long workshop, teachers were to tour the museum. We wanted them to see this excellent, but under-utilized, local resource that was perfect for field trips.

My workshop room was on the first floor, just down the hall from the museum's gift shop. On our first break, many teachers browsed the shop, but very few made a purchase. Later in the day, we discussed the power of adding hooks to presentations and began to actively engage in the creative process. During the next break, the teachers went back into the shop. On this visit, they viewed almost every item as a potential prop for a lesson or a creative way to engage the class. Multiple teachers came up to me over the three days to show me what they had purchased and explain how they planned to use it. Teachers walked out of the museum each evening carrying gift shop bags filled with all sorts of strange items. I should have received a commission!

What changed between their first visit to the gift shop when nothing seemed interesting, and the next visit when everything held potential as a prop or classroom tool? The inventory didn't change. In fact, the exact items were in the shop the first time the teachers walked through; those items just didn't register as significant or related to them. *After* engaging in the creative process, the same teachers experienced the world in a completely different way. By changing their focus and activating the creative genius that resides inside each of us, they were transported into a world of abundance; one where incredible ideas were all around them for the taking.

The same thing can happen for you. Creativity is rarely about natural brilliance or innate genius. Much more often creativity results from properly directed attention, laser-like focus, relentless effort, and hard work. Outsiders see the glorious results but know very little about the blood and sweat that happens behind closed doors. Creative genius is something people tend to romanticize, but the reality is not very romantic at all. Like any skill it takes practice and effort. No one assumes that an accomplished doctor, rocket scientist, or engineer "lucked" their way into greatness. We have a certain understanding and appreciation for the years of study, sacrifice, and hard work it takes for these experts to reach the highest levels of their profession. Yet when we see accomplished artists and exceptionally creative people, we jump to the conclusion that their talent is God-given or natural. Most people would be surprised to pull back the curtain and see the years of excruciating labor, relentless pursuit of excellence, and monstrous obstacles those "naturals" have overcome.

THE 6 WORDS

Any time I speak to a group of educators, whether it is a workshop, keynote address, or conference session, I tell the following story. You almost have to hear it live for it to have its full impact and intensity. I am a very passionate and enthusiastic speaker, but when I tell this story, my energy and intensity ramps up to astronomical levels. Afterwards, if people talk to me about a story from the day it is inevitably this one. My book wouldn't be complete without an attempt to share this story. I hope I can do it justice.

Several years ago, a former colleague asked me for some advice. We were teaching many of the same students and she was having a very difficult time with behavior management— and just about everything else.

"If people knew how hard I had to work to gain my mastery, it wouldn't seem so wonderful at all."
MICHELANGELO

When I say she was struggling, I mean she was close to having a breakdown and flat out leaving the profession. She knew from the constant buzz about my class that I was having success with these same students, so she asked if we could discuss some of my techniques and strategies.

Well, I love to discuss these ideas with fellow teachers so my answer was an automatic "Yes." We met the next day, and within the first five minutes of our conversation she said the six words that got me unbelievably fired up. Using only six words she said two very sinister things that carry very serious implications. Now, when she said the six words, I said "Thank you," because she was giving me credit for a very desirable character trait. It wasn't until later that I realized why I had such an uncomfortable response to her six words. Walking away from that meeting, the disturbing nature of those six words suddenly hit me and I immediately realized why I had such a visceral reaction to them. Apparently, you can say a lot in six words.

(Right about now, some of you are ready to scream, "Just tell me the six words!" If you were listening to the story live, you'd be ready to shake the words out of me. It is worth pointing out this reaction is not unintentional. The building up of the story incorporates elements of classic storytelling technique. First, a preview to the story explains its importance and impact in a way that hopefully helps to build anticipation. Then, the most essential element of the story, the six words, is strategically kept from you. The story could begin with the six words but I have made a presentational decision to not reveal them until later in the story in an effort to build dramatic tension. All of these elements are examples of what can be done when presenting content in the classroom. What a great place to be in where your audience is ready to strangle you if you don't tell them the very content that you are trying so desperately to deliver. It changes the positioning of the situation and creates an entirely different dynamic. Now, back to the six words!)

The six words were…now, when I tell you the six words, some of you will think they aren't such a big deal, but some of you will get it right away. Hopefully, by the end of this story, it will sink in for everyone.

She said, "It's easy for you. You're creative."

Wow! Let me repeat that. "It's easy for you. You're creative."

The first sinister implication can be found in the first four words, "It's easy for you."

It's easy for me. Really? So with four words she dismissed *sixteen years* of hard work! Sixteen years of brainstorming. Sixteen years' worth of notebook after notebook filled with ideas, most of which sucked! Sixteen years of failures and lessons that blew up in my face. Sixteen years of fine-tuning ideas and making adjustments because what I thought were great ideas went completely wrong. Sixteen years of having to abandon lessons part way through the day in order to salvage something useful.

I've worked my butt off to build a class that is outrageously engaging, fun, educationally sound, and dearly loved by students. It wasn't easy when I started, it wasn't easy last week, and it won't be easy next week either. It's not supposed to be easy—it's supposed to be worth it. You can build something incredible if you put the effort in on the front end, and then keep putting the effort in until you turn the lights off and close your door for the last time. But it won't be *"easy."*

The risk faced by anyone who has achieved a high level of skill and polish in any particular field is that since they make it look so easy, some will assume it was. I'm convinced the concept of "the natural" is entirely erroneous. It's only through relentless practice that these professionals can fool you into believing it to be so.

The second sinister implication can be found in words five and six.

"You're creative."

What is she implying by that?

She is implying two things. First, she is implying I have some sort of inborn character trait known as creativity. Secondly, and more importantly, she is implying she is *not* creative. She wasn't given this particular trait, so she is excused from doing the same hard work I put in! Her lack of "natural" creative ability therefore excuses her for the fact that her class sucks! It excuses her from the fact that kids aren't learning successfully and reaching their potential in her class. And, she gets a pass on the fact that students leave her class with *less* of a love of learning than when they started.

Oh, no she doesn't. It's not OK to throw up your hands in defeat because you're not naturally creative. Few, if any, teachers are innately creative. I know I'm being harsh, but I'm trying to make an important point. Education can be used to uplift and inspire or it can be used as a hammer to bludgeon and beat down. We must collectively agree educating the next generation is worth the time and effort and that our students deserve to be uplifted and inspired. Creativity is not the possession of some special class of artistic individuals, but is rather something that can be nurtured and developed in all of us—including your students!

> *"Some critics will write 'Maya Angelou is a natural writer,' which is right after being a natural heart surgeon."*
> MAYA ANGELOU

As a disclaimer, the teacher I am referring to is a very nice woman who cares deeply about kids and was honestly trying to get better at her profession. She would be horrified to think that she was implying these things and, I'm positive, meant no offense. That's why I thanked her and we continued to make some real strides forward. I'm one hundred percent behind anyone who wants to improve, and I applaud her for caring enough to seek guidance and taking the risk of asking me for assistance.

BUT...I know I have to keep telling this story. Why? Because too many teachers use those six words as an excuse. Case in point: I visited with several teachers following a conference session in Monterey, California, when one of them (Thank you, Mary!) gave me some interesting insight. She had been in the women's bathroom immediately after the session and overheard several ladies discussing my session. One of the ladies mentioned the "six words" story and said that it felt like a punch to her stomach. Up to that point in the session, she had been sitting there thinking to herself the exact same thing, "Easy for him, he's the creative magician guy. I could never pull this stuff off." Hearing the story, she realized I was talking about her. It challenged her to reconsider her belief that creativity is something you either have or don't have. Because she could relate to the six words and realized their fallacy, she was willing to step outside her comfort zone and give some of my methods a shot.

That's all I'm asking for, an open mind and the willingness to suspend disbelief in your creative ability. Have faith that what I'm telling you is true. We all have unbelievable creative potential. It lies dormant just waiting—no *begging*—to be tapped. I haven't presented a workshop or keynote address since that day without including the "six words." I can't tell you how many people have come up to me and said they appreciated the story because they have heard similar sentiments expressed to them. Don't doubt for a minute that you are a creative wellspring that will soon be releasing a flood of awesome ideas into the world.

THE REAL LAW OF ATTRACTION

I have to come clean. I lied to you when I told you that the "blinding flash of light" theory about creativity is a myth. It really isn't a myth. You absolutely *will* receive creative inspirations out of nowhere and at the oddest times, but you will only get them if you put in the work on the front end. Those flashes of inspiration will only come when you have "tuned" your mind to the correct frequency by engaging in the creative process and asking the right questions. Don't be frustrated by a lack of results in a brainstorming session or while trying to add creative presentational hooks to your lessons. Participating in the process and creating a vision of the outrageously high engagement level you desire from your students is the necessary first step. Then, and only then, you will be stunned by the fact that your brain will continue to work overtime, consciously and subconsciously, to fulfill your goals and vision. When you ask the right questions, your brain won't be satisfied until it has provided the answers.

Remember, the quality of your questions is critical. Don't ask, "How can I make this lesson bearable for my students today and keep them awake?" unless you want an answer that requires the bare minimum. Instead ask, "How can I make this lesson outrageously entertaining, engaging, and powerful so that my students will never forget it and will be desperate to come back for more?" That is a qualitatively different question and will lead to a qualitatively different answer. Your brain won't be satisfied until it has received a proper and fitting response.

My problem with many interpretations of the Law of Attraction is that it makes it sound like you just wish for a new car and someone drives one into your driveway and gives it to you. It doesn't work like that. To put the real Law of Attraction to work for you, you must create a vision of what you want and define the goals you want to achieve—and then you must start *working* for them. Once you have a vision and fixed a destination *and* started out after it, you will be shocked at how much assistance you receive along the way. As William H. Murray poignantly said,

> "Until one is committed there is hesitancy, the chance to draw back, always ineffectiveness. Concerning all acts of initiative (and creation), there is one elementary truth the ignorance of which kills countless ideas and splendid plans: that the moment one definitely commits oneself, the providence moves too. A whole stream of events issues from the decision, raising in one's favor all manner of unforeseen incidents, meetings and material assistance, which no man could have dreamt would have come his way."

Commit. Start working. Then, be open. Recognize this providential assistance when it comes, and leap to take advantage of it. Don't dismiss the ideas that your brain is trying to send you. Many people are on the receiving end of incredible amounts of creative ideas but either don't recognize them as such or don't have the confidence to act. Ideas are great, but implementation is the key to results. In my all-day version of the *Outrageous Teaching* seminar, as well as my Teaching Outside the Box workshop, teachers spend time working collaboratively to brainstorm ideas for their own lessons. They use a creativity tool I developed called "The Ultimate, Kick Butt, No-Holds-Barred, Super Turbo-Charged Lesson Plan Brainstorming Power Pack System!" (Sorry, sometimes my inner-copywriter gets the best of me!) I have seen unbelievably creative lesson plan ideas come out of these sessions; ideas that are all for naught unless those teachers follow through on the next steps of the creative process. To make a difference in your classroom, your ideas must be developed and then, ultimately, implemented in front of students. Based on feedback from teachers across the nation, I know many of these ideas and strategies have found their way off the brainstorming page and into classrooms where they belong. I still remember getting an email, complete with pictures, from Mary Bears-Sylvia, a teacher who attended a one-hour, super-abbreviated *Outrageous Teaching* conference session. She received creative inspiration and had the courage to run with it. She came up with her idea, developed it, and brought it to fruition in her classroom *two days* after the conference. That's implementation!

You have probably heard the story about the man who stood on his roof during a flood and waited for God to save him. A rescue boat came to get him and he said he was fine and that God would help him. Another rescue boat came and begged him to get in but he rejected the help. Finally a helicopter flew overhead and dropped a ladder to him but he refused to go, proclaiming his faith in the Lord. The waters topped his roof and he drowned. Upon entering heaven he was indignant and confronted God, "How could you let me die up there on that roof after all the faith I've had in you?" God replied, "Come on, I sent you two boats and a helicopter!" Don't be that guy. Jump on creative ideas and opportunities that come your way, and then implement them! Be proactive in your pursuit of your vision for your classroom and life. The Law of Attraction is real. Your thoughts are magical and have the power to manifest your dreams but *not* without your active participation in the process.

DESIGN A SYSTEM TO CAPTURE IDEAS

Your subconscious mind does not work at the same pace as your conscious mind. Brilliant ideas will come to you in the strangest of circumstances. They will come to you in the shower, at the gym, and while driving in your car. They will hit you in the grocery store, on a walk, and while getting a haircut. Some of my best ideas come while doing the dishes, cleaning the house, or during other activities when the conscious brain is on auto-pilot. Since these ideas often surface at odd times, you'll want to be perpetually prepared to capture them. Don't say, "I'll write that down when I get home." You won't! In fact you likely won't even remember you had an idea in the first place. Instead, create a system for immediately capturing and organizing your ideas so they are not lost forever.

I get sick to my stomach when I think of all of the ideas I have lost because I was sure I would remember them. Sometimes I'll see an ex-student and they'll mention something they remember from a class years ago. Inevitably I think, "Why don't I do that anymore?" I don't do it because I didn't write it down and forgot how powerful that particular element was to the lesson.

To prevent idea evaporation, I developed a habit years ago of traveling with an index card and a pen in my pocket at all times. I used these to jot down thoughts and ideas I wanted to remember. When I emptied my pockets each evening, I put the notes where I could find them later (a file, notebook, etc.). Now that I have a smartphone with me at all times, I have transitioned to using a note-taking app for the same purpose. There are any number of amazing apps, such as Evernote, that can assist in capturing and organizing your ideas. Whatever system you choose, just make sure it's always available to you and that you actually use it. Don't buy some fancy organizational notebook or buy some complicated app that you will never use. The simpler your idea-capture system is, the better. Choose practicality over flash.

Your system doesn't have to be high-tech. I tend to create a manila file folder or a three-ring notebook for any project I'm working on. I still have the notebook I used when I first developed the original *Outrageous Teaching* seminar and the whole PIRATE mnemonic. It has tabs for each letter and is filled with random thoughts, ideas, and brainstorming results. I filled the pockets with index cards and scraps of paper with quotes and reminders. Years later, I can look back and see all of the possibilities I considered when generating the *Teach Like a PIRATE* system.

MAKE IT EASY

The point of your idea-capture system, as well as the implementation of those ideas, is to keep it simple and easily accessible. The more steps you are required to do before you can actually be productive, the less likely it is that you will be consistently successful. This is true of fitness programs as well, by the way. One study found that the distance of your workout facility directly correlates to how frequently you use it. The greater the distance, the less likely you are to go to the gym on a daily basis. I know for me, the single biggest change I originally made when I began to lose 40 pounds of excess weight was to walk. The reason was simple: all I had to do was open my door and go. Whatever system you develop to record your ideas, organize your thoughts, and develop your plans for implementation, make sure it is quick and easy to use.

For me to get this book written, I decided to take my own advice. I invested in a Mac Air which gave me the portability to work anywhere. When I was tied to my desktop and a particular space, I was far less successful. Now I can write on planes, in any room in the house (important when you have young children), literally anywhere in the world. I am writing these very words on a Spring Break vacation in Puerto Vallarta, Mexico. The easier you make it to work, the more likely you will.

Developing a system to capture your ideas has an additional benefit. You are telling yourself that you are, indeed, going to get some creative insights. This can become a self-fulfilling prophecy. Capturing your thoughts validates their worth, an act that sends the subtle but powerful message to your subconscious that the effort spent on idea generation won't be squandered.

FAILURE VS. FEEDBACK

I mentioned earlier that I have had lessons blow up in my face and a long series of failures in the classroom. It's absolutely true! I have had legendary failures. I have had out and out disasters occur as I have tried to develop and implement my ideas. I'm not even completely satisfied with all of my lessons from last week because I know they could have been better.

> *"Only those who risk going too far can possibly find out how far they can go."*
>
> T.S. ELIOT

It goes with the territory.

If you haven't failed in the classroom lately, you aren't pushing the envelope far enough. "Safe" lessons are a recipe for mediocrity at best.

The key to failing without quitting is to shift your paradigm to believe there is no such thing as true failure—only feedback. When you have a vision for how you want your class to be, you can then analyze the results. Use those results, a.k.a. feedback, for improvement. For example, if you notice that your class is not engaged by your presentation, it isn't helpful or empowering to blame your students. Obviously, if they're not engaged, they are providing you with some critical feedback: what you are doing is not engaging for this audience, on this day. Try to evaluate and learn from that feedback, without taking it too personally. Doing so will allow you to make adjustments and improve your future presentations. The truly skilled practitioner has the sensory acuity to read the audience's engagement level and make real-time adjustments on the fly. That's the ultimate goal and, although difficult, it is attainable. Don't get so wrapped up in what you are doing and what is listed next on your agenda that you fail to see the feedback that is being constantly provided by your audience.

I still remember reading *Psycho-Cybernetics*, by Maxwell Maltz, as a youngster. His comparison of the way humans attain their goals to the way missiles and torpedoes hit their targets had a profound impact on me. Dr. Maltz said, "The torpedo accomplishes its goal by going forward, making errors, and continually correcting them. By a series of zigzags it literally gropes its way to the goal." In fact, the missile is likely to be off target a far greater percentage of the time than it is on target. Nevertheless, it arrives and hits its target because of the constant adjustments made based on continual analysis of the feedback provided. Similarly, the path to great teaching looks like instructions for washing your hair: Try, fail, adjust, try, fail, adjust...lather, rinse, repeat.

> *"Only those who dare to fail greatly can ever achieve greatly."*
> ROBERT F. KENNEDY

After a recent seminar presentation, a woman approached me and thanked me for admitting I still fail. She said she found it intimidating to listen to professional-development speakers who make it sound as if their classes are perfect. These speakers don't let on that they experience the trials and tribulations we all know are a part of this (heck, any!) profession. Perhaps they are concerned that they'll lose credibility by showing vulnerability, but they are completely wrong. My goal is to provide a realistic look into the classroom and that simply can't be done without talking about failure.

In my opinion, any endeavor that doesn't hold the possibility of failure can't accomplish anything meaningful. The idea of the perfect school year doesn't (thank God!) exist. Don't let that stop you from attempting something new. Instead, be encouraged to push the edge and reach new heights. Just bring lots of bandages for the knees you are going to scrape along the way.

CREATIVE ALCHEMY

Becoming well-read and involved in a wide variety of interests provides us with the raw resources that we need for what I call Creative Alchemy. Too often, people believe creativity is some esoteric skill that involves coming up with completely original ideas from out of the blue. That is rarely the way it works. I liken real creativity more to these definitions of alchemy.

Alchemy:

1. *The magical process of transmuting a common substance, usually of little value, into a substance of great value.*

2. *A process by which paradoxical results are achieved by the combination of incompatible elements.*

Spend more time on your passions, hobbies, and outside areas of interest and then seek ways to incorporate them into your classroom. Cultivate new hobbies and watch new areas of your brain explode in creative output. Watch your life light up with a new energy as you rekindle the feelings you had for the passions of your younger days. Grow! Try new things and do those bucket-list items. Notice the world around you and treat it like the bountiful supply of creative ideas that it is. It's not just good for your life...it's great for your teaching. Exploring the world and your passions allows you to bring a new perspective and energy into the classroom. It allows you to become a powerful role model for your students. We always say we want them to be life-long learners, so we must show them what that looks like.

Creative stagnation is often a result of:

1. Being unwilling to venture outside of our expertise.

2. An inability to see how seemingly unrelated ideas can be combined into something new and powerful.

I believe the best books to read about teaching are rarely in the education section. I always have three or four books on my nightstand, a book in my car, one in my school bag, and several more on my phone. I consider it one of the most important parts of my job to constantly expose myself to the high quality thinking of other people. It challenges me, it keeps me current, and it provides me the raw resources necessary for creative alchemy.

My outside interests are wide, varied, and growing. Here are some examples: magic, origami, chess, coaching basketball, fitness, entrepreneurship, direct marketing, social media, rap music, success literature, public speaking, civil rights, and most recently, the Rubik's Cube. When I only focus on my teaching, I am not nearly as creative as when I find time to humor my strange obsessions.

Examples of creative alchemy are everywhere. Jazz was made through creative alchemy. Rock n' roll...creative alchemy. Rap music...creative alchemy. Forgive me for dating myself, but I still remember when Run DMC added a rock guitar to many of their rap songs and created a new sound.

Artists increase their creativity by experimenting with different mediums. Musicians experience watershed moments of creativity after becoming influenced by other bands, artists, and styles. Marketers design brilliant campaigns after exposing themselves to methods of other industries and then seeking to apply the ideas to their own.

Here is alchemy at work:

1. For years I have incorporated origami (one of my outside interests) into my history class, but I was always frustrated that I had no use for the narrow strip of paper left over after cutting two hundred 8 ½" x 11 ½" pieces of paper into a square.

2. I have also been frustrated for the past few years with my 1920s Henry Ford assembly line simulation. I didn't like the final product of the activity and had, in fact, stopped doing it for a couple of years.

3. A couple of years ago, I saw a student create a "helicopter" out of a narrow piece of paper. I asked him to teach it to me and I put it in my file of ideas to use at some point in the future.

After two years...I repeat, two years...the creative alchemy finally worked its magic. (How long should you wait for a good idea? As long as it takes!) Now, I use the strips of paper for the raw materials that I need to turn each class into several competing teams of helicopter-making assembly lines during my Henry Ford lesson. I solved the answer to my wasted strips of paper problem, my assembly line problem, and the problem of how to use the cool principle taught to me by a student. This semester was my first attempt, and I think it is going to be a keeper. Alchemy!

Don't fall into the trap of thinking time spent developing yourself into a well-rounded person, above and beyond your role as an educator, is wasted or something to feel guilty about. It is *essential* and will pay dividends in not only your life, but also in your classroom.

TRANSFORMATION

"Provide an uncommon experience for your students and they will reward you with an uncommon effort and attitude."

DAVE BURGESS

For many students, school is filled with monotony, drudgery, and soul-killing suckiness. When I think about a student's typical school day, it makes me completely understand why so many of them don't want to be there. Too often school is a place where creativity is systematically killed, individuality is stamped out, and boredom reigns supreme. There are really only two possibilities; either your class can be a reprieve from all of that or it can be a contributing factor. I am thoroughly committed to having my class be a reprieve.

I want my class to stand out in the sea of sameness that is the educational landscape. I want my class to be, as Seth Godin says, a Purple Cow. In his book by the same title, Seth writes, "Something remarkable is worth talking about. Worth noticing. Exceptional. New. Interesting. It's a Purple Cow. Boring stuff is invisible. It's a brown cow." Although his book was written for marketers, it validates much of what I believe is true in teaching.

Students are hit with so much information and stimuli every day that to stand out in their minds, you must be remarkable. *Remarkable* means that you are so exceptional and different that people talk about you—in a good way. Being merely good doesn't cut it; you have to be extraordinary. I am always shooting to have the most talked about class on campus and the conference session with the most buzz. That goal isn't about ego, it's about *effectiveness*.

Standing out from the crowd is the only way to guarantee your message is received in a culture that is increasingly distracted and where attention spans are plummeting. If you feel your message is important, and I do, it is worth the effort to go to any lengths to make sure it is successfully delivered.

Too many schools are filled with brown cow classes that blend into the background. I am relentlessly focused and immersed in the orchestrated effort to be the antithesis of the brown cow. I want entering my room to feel like entering another world. Many years ago, I wrote out how I want my class to be viewed by my students. Written through the eyes of a fictional student, it is reflective of letters and comments I have received from actual students.

> "As I walked in to SS-9 as a new student in Mr. Burgess' class, I was filled with an overwhelming sense of anticipation. I'd heard about his reputation, I'd heard my peers tell all of the strange stories, and I most certainly had seen his over-the-top costumes as he paraded around campus. There was no possible way that he could live up to all of the hype, and yet, after a few weeks, I realized that Mr. Burgess was even better than advertised.
>
> I have never seen such a consistent level of enthusiasm from a teacher, or anyone else for that matter. This man has a passion for teaching. He is a larger-than-life superhuman mix of educator, psychologist, historian, magician, stand-up comic, and

certified lunatic! Some days I feel I should have to pay admission to see his lesson, and every day I am amazed that I have learned so much! I only hope to find something to do with my life that brings me that much joy and fulfillment.

One thing is certain, learning history has never been this much fun or this easy. I don't mean easy as in we don't have to learn a lot, I mean easy as in I notice that I'm retaining all of the content without my usual struggles. It must be that brain-based research and those mnemonics that Mr. Burgess told us about at the beginning of the year. I have even noticed that some of my friends who always seem to fail the classes we have together understand the material. It's really strange, these are the same kids that are getting in trouble and having confrontations with teachers in my other classes and yet here they thrive. It's almost like the air is easier to breathe in SS-9. I'm going to be honest with you…some days this class is the only reason I come to school."

THE WORLD'S GREATEST GPS…YOUR BRAIN

I found this letter-writing exercise to be extremely valuable, and it's something I recommend you consider trying for yourself. It allowed me to construct a vision of what I want students to experience in my class. It serves as the ideal goal that I'm shooting for as I proceed through my career. When I lack motivation or inspiration, I re-read this passage and re-dedicate myself to fulfilling the vision.

When embarking on any journey, choosing the destination is a critical first step. With a destination in mind, you can set your internal GPS and be assured you are heading in the correct direction. It makes no sense at all to drive the streets of your city getting further and further lost and increasingly frustrated, and then have the nerve to blame your expensive GPS system when, actually, you never entered a destination. You have to have a vision of what your ideal classroom experience looks like if you want to have any hope of creating it.

In addition to a specific destination, you must also have an accurate view of the current reality of your class. A GPS doesn't work unless the system can determine your precise current location and its maps are up to date. When you have a realistic view of your current classroom and can see where it falls short of your ultimate vision, you have something to work with.

In his wonderful book, *Creating*, Robert Fritz describes how this gap between current reality and vision creates a certain tension. If you are truly committed to fulfilling your vision, this tension will drive you to constantly work to close the gap. Knowing that you aren't living up to the standard you've set for yourself feels uncomfortable. Therefore, it is extremely motivating and rewarding to move towards resolving this dissonance.

TWO QUESTIONS FOR RAISING THE BAR

I often ask my seminar participants to consider their answers to the following two questions. For many, acknowledging the truth is somewhat painful. I hope you'll take a few minutes to answer these questions for yourself. The purpose here is to get you to consider your expectations and standards for what is possible in a classroom.

Question One: If your students didn't have to be there, would you be teaching in an empty room?

In other words, if, like some college courses, there were no attendance requirements and no consequences for missing class, and your students were only held responsible for passing the tests, would they still show up every day for *your* class? Is there something about you and the experience of being a part of your class that would draw students in? Have you created an environment that is so unique and so enjoyable that students are pulled into your room as if by a magnet? Is your class so engaging that students would show up on a Saturday if you invited them to come in for a special lesson opportunity? Are students rescheduling doctor appointments and trips off campus to avoid missing your class? Do they make their parents bring them back after appointments in the hopes of still catching your period? Do students wait to go to the bathroom until their next period because they are afraid they will miss something unforgettable in your room? Do you have students trying to ditch their other periods because they want to be a part of your lesson more than once? Do they try to bring their friends into your class so that they can have the experience? Will they create havoc in the counseling office if they get their schedule changed and moved to another teacher (even though that teacher might be awesome as well)? Do they try to sneak back on campus after graduation in order to participate in certain lessons again? Do they talk about things that happened in your class years afterward? When you see them the next year do they sincerely express how much they miss your class?

Question Two: Do you have any lessons you could sell tickets for?

Wow! Now that is really raising the bar. I'll honestly tell you that I don't have a lot of those, but I do have some! The Lunar Landing Lesson for sure. Maybe the 60s Party, the Speakeasy, and the day the Red Scare super villain comes to school. Probably, the Salem Witchcraft Trials, the Trail of Tears, and the day the 10-Man teaches the Bill of Rights. I sincerely believe there are days I could have a cash register outside of the door and students would pay a small sum of money to come in. I'm trying to create as many of those days as I possibly can and sprinkle them throughout the school year.

I don't really expect teachers to be able to answer yes to both questions (especially the second) for every one of their lessons. But I do want them—and you—to use these questions to create a "bar-raising" paradigm shift. So, how is it possible to transform your class to the point where you can answer yes to the preceding questions? One way I try to do it is by attempting to blur the lines between education and entertainment. I stopped using the term "edutainment" because it became a bit of a cliché, but I still believe it is a fairly accurate term for my classroom. My goal is to, at least sometimes, have students asking themselves, "Is this a lesson I walked into or is it a show?" When I'm presenting content, I attempt to draw on tried and true principles of staging and showmanship in order to turn my lesson into an event…an extravaganza. In Section II of this book, I provide great detail on how to incorporate naturally engaging elements into your class on a daily basis and provide sound reasoning why entertainment and fun can, and should, go hand in hand with learning. The goal is to transform your class into something irresistible to your students.

POSITIONING AND REFRAMING

Proper positioning is one of the key techniques needed to effectively transform your class into a powerful, must-be place. Positioning is a marketing term that was made famous by Al Ries and Jack Trout in their groundbreaking book, *Positioning: The Battle for Your Mind*. It is the process by which you create a compelling picture and understanding in the minds of your audience members to differentiate your brand, product, or service.

For example, Wal-Mart is positioned as the place to go for huge selection and low prices. On the other hand, Nordstrom is positioned as a place for high-end shopping and extraordinary customer service. Zappos built a business by using legendary (remarkable) customer service to generate word-of-mouth referrals and loyal customers. Prius is positioned as the "green" alternative for those who are environmentally conscious. You can send a package with any number of services, but where would you go if it "absolutely, positively, had to be there overnight?" Federal Express built a business by positioning itself through speed of delivery. I've heard the direct marketing genius Dan Kennedy speak about the USP (Unique Selling Proposition) of Domino's Pizza many times. The original positioning statement was "Fresh, Hot Pizza Delivered in 30 minutes or Less…Guaranteed." By positioning themselves this way they literally created a category that didn't exist and dominated it for a long time. They didn't say they had the best pizza but if you were a starving college student who wanted a pizza fast you knew exactly who to call.

I think you get the idea. So, what does positioning have to do with teaching? Well, again, I turn to a question I learned from Dan Kennedy's Magnetic Marketing program. It's a question marketers must answer for potential clients: "Why should I do business with you out of all of the possible choices in your category?" To succeed in business, you must position yourself in the marketplace so you are the clear choice amongst all alternatives and against the alternative of doing nothing at all. This is exactly what we must do as teachers, as well! Why should our students bother to learn what we are teaching? Why should they bother to give us their attention and active engagement in the first place? Because here's the truth: Not only are we fighting to stand out from all the images, sounds, products, people, and emotions vying for their attention, we are also fighting to keep them from tuning out altogether.

It isn't easy. There's a lot of noise out there and let's face it, it's hard for our subjects to compete with the excitement of their favorite reality show or real-life drama in the halls. It's easy to see why so many teachers use what I call "the medicine approach." They say, "I know this stuff is hard but you have to bear with me and hang in there because it's on the test." "I know this is rough going and not exactly fun but if you don't learn this stuff you can't be successful at the next level." Talk about piss-poor motivation! Suffer through this grueling ordeal so that you can answer a few more questions right on the state test. They are positioning their lesson like it is bitter medicine that must be swallowed in order to get better.

Don't position your material as if it is awful-tasting medicine! Position your content as if it's amazing! Give motivating reasons why the material is important to know. "Because it's on the test" doesn't cut it. If you can't explain why someone should pay attention to what you're saying, maybe you shouldn't be saying it.

I go out of my way to position my class as an amazing and extraordinarily unique place filled with outrageously engaging content and activities. I position it as a place that provides opportunities for creative expression. I also try to position each lesson so students can personalize the material and apply it to their world. I add in the LCLs (life-changing lessons) in an attempt to make my class fulfilling and meaningful. Then, when appropriate, I add in the entertainment and fun factor to top it all off. I design my lessons so that even the tough material goes down easy, much like the pet owner who hides the pill inside of a tasty morsel. And I don't apologize for utilizing all of the tricks of the trade to accomplish my goals.

Sometimes we need to change our students' perceptions of the material we're teaching. The way to do this is called reframing. Reframing involves providing a new context for the material that helps to break down the negative associations many students come into class with. I'm sure you've heard students saying things like, "I hate math." "History is boring." "I can't write." "I'll never need to know this in real life." These are some of the preconceived notions our students bring with them to school. Our job is to create a mental paradigm shift by reframing the content and its value and relevancy to their lives.

The truth is, students probably don't really hate math, they hate the way it has been taught to them in the past. They hate the fact that they have struggled to learn math in the past. They think history is boring because a teacher somewhere along the way killed it with dreary bookwork, worksheets, and monotonous lectures. History isn't boring, their history *class* was. When students can't see any real-world connection or value to a particular subject, they question whether it is worth the investment and effort. And rightly so! As adults, we don't like to feel that our time and efforts are being wasted; students are no different.

The following story is my favorite example of the power of reframing. When my son was about five or six years old, I took him to a pizza place with two other families. It was one of those places with a small game area for children. This one also had about five of those gumball-type vending machines that spit out prizes (stickers, small toys, temporary tattoos, etc.) rather than gum. My son, Hayden, and two of his buddies approached the machines excitedly with quarters in hand. The first friend put his money in and got a small, plastic, glow-in-the-dark T-Rex. He ran off displaying it proudly and making loud roaring noises as he went. The second friend pulled the lever and got a temporary tattoo of a fire-breathing dragon. He grabbed his father and dragged him into the bathroom to immediately apply it to his arm with water from the sink. Finally, Hayden approached the machines and carefully chose where to place his quarters. He pushed and pulled and out came a small plastic capsule with something inside. He handed it to me to pry the top off and out came a small gold bracelet with heart charms. Disaster!! I knew I had about a half second to reframe this experience for my son or there could be a legendary meltdown. After all, a heart bracelet is a devastating prize for a young boy when compared to a T-Rex and a fire-breathing dragon tattoo. I'm not always so quick on my feet in such circumstances, but this time, without any hesitation, I held it up, pointed to it, and emphatically yelled, "Pirate treasure!!!" He grabbed it from me and ran off clutching it yelling, "Yeaaahh!!" at the top of his lungs.

That is reframing. Sometimes the most important thing we do as teachers is to take subjects, which to a lot of our students start as the equivalent of little heart bracelets, and by using passion, enthusiasm, powerful presentations, and creativity, turn it into pirate treasure. The entire *Teach Like a PIRATE* system is tailor-made to help make that transformation possible.

ENTHUSIASM

"Nothing great was ever achieved without enthusiasm."

RALPH WALDO EMERSON

"There is nothing more contagious on this planet than enthusiasm. The songs become incidental, what people receive is your joy."

CARLOS SANTANA

"If the body leads, the brain will follow."

DAVE BURGESS

It is no accident that the cornerstones of the *Teach Like a PIRATE* system are Passion and Enthusiasm. I believe excellence as a teacher starts with having passion for what you do in life, and is driven home with your enthusiasm. Enthusiasm is the closer that comes into the game in the ninth inning and finishes it off. If you apply nothing else from this book, but you consistently ramp up your enthusiasm level in the classroom, you will be far ahead of the game and a dramatically better teacher. Enthusiasm is that important.

Even on the days when some students may not be enthralled with the subject matter, they are engaged by, if nothing else, the fact that I am *wound up* and *going off!* The ability to perceive the ebb and flow of engagement in the classroom, and then counter with an adjustment in enthusiasm, is a skill that is almost impossible to quantify and tough to teach. It's a skill that separates good teachers from great ones. I'll always choose a teacher with enthusiasm and weak technique over one with brilliant strategies but who is just punching the clock. Why? An enthusiastic teacher can learn technique, method, and strategy, but it is almost impossible to light a fire inside the charred heart of a burned-out teacher.

THE COMMITMENT TO BEING "ON"

Confession time! As an educator, there are a lot of things I'm not good at. I don't always grade promptly or provide quick and meaningful feedback to my students. I tend to let papers and projects pile up, which means I eventually tackle them without the same attention to detail I would have if I graded more consistently. I'm not good at organizing and implementing long-term group projects. When my students work collaboratively, I'm not great at parsing out credit in a way that is fair to everybody. I haven't figured out the perfect system to deal with those situations when one or two students do the majority of the work and some are freeloaders. I'm still working out how to teach my students to take meaningful notes. I could get a lot better at incorporating technology in my classroom, especially in the hands of students. My list of inadequacies in the classroom could go on to such embarrassing lengths that you would begin to wonder why I could have possibly thought myself worthy of writing a book on teaching. Sixteen years into the game and I'm still a work in progress.

Despite all my shortcomings, I know I excel in one important area: enthusiasm. I pride myself on flat out *bringing it* whether I'm teaching a class of students or leading a seminar for teachers. I am absolutely committed to being "on" every period of the day. If you walk into my room during first period and then come back for sixth period at the end of the day, you will see the same intensity in my presentation both times. I pride myself on that almost more than anything else I do.

In part, I think my ability to be "on" is a byproduct of my experience as a magician. Most magicians, and I'm no exception, get their first paid gigs as children's performers at birthday parties. I have the utmost respect for magicians who effectively work this market; it is tough work! Performers who are weak or lack audience-engagement skills get eaten alive. Sounds like teaching doesn't it? The gig is sort of like being a permanent substitute teacher—one of the toughest assignments in the educational world. To top it off, almost all of the shows are on Saturdays and Sundays, and a busy performer might have four or five shows a day. By the fourth or fifth show, it would be easy to just go through the motions as you perform the same tricks all over again. But, as a professional, you can't. If for no other reason, you know someone is standing at the back of the room with her checkbook in hand. She is the mother. You are being paid for *this* performance; she could care less that her child's party is your fifth of the day. This is the only sixth birthday party her child will ever have. It is the only time many people in the crowd will actually see a professional magician perform live right in front of them. They will judge whether magic is an art form worthy of paid performance at other venues based in part on what you do in that moment. Professional performers feel a huge weight of responsibility to deliver something special for this particular audience on this particular day. What you've done before in your day, or your career, doesn't matter a bit. You have to bring it *now*!

Teaching is exactly like that. I might be the only person who ever talks to my students about Malcolm X in their whole life. I refuse to cheat a student by delivering a subpar performance just because he has me later in the day, or early in the day when I'm not quite awake. Although no mother stands in the back of the room with a checkbook, in a very real sense, I know forty mothers and a whole community are counting on me. That's why, if you are my student or you come to my workshop I personally guarantee I won't cheat you in the enthusiasm department. Even if you are the only person in the room, I'm going to flat out bring it.

It isn't easy for anyone to be "on" *every time* they're in front of an audience. Les Brown shares a story in his *The Power of Purpose* audio program about getting a late night call from a young man who had come to hear him speak and felt Les hadn't given his best. Les offered all kinds of excuses—complaints about the circumstances surrounding the event, unfulfilled promises of the promoters, the small crowd size—but the kid wouldn't let him off the hook. Finally, Les relented when the kid threw his own line back in his face. *"You said, 'We must deal with circumstances such as we find them!'"* I have never forgotten that story and have vowed that, although I will do my best to create ideal circumstances, I will not allow that which is outside my control to affect my effort and enthusiasm.

I have walked into some amazingly challenging scenarios as I have traveled around giving professional development workshops and keynotes. I never know what I'll find. I once presented in a converted hotel room with seventy-plus people packed in everywhere, including sitting on the floor directly behind me. My colleague Reuben Hoffman was in the hall packing more and more in. (We broke a lot of fire codes that day!) On the other hand, I have presented, with no amplification, to tiny groups spread out over huge gymnasiums. Neither situation is ideal, but I repeat Les' line in my head, "You must deal with circumstances such as you find them." My job is to put myself in a powerful state and do my best to rock the house.

TWO WAYS TO LIGHT YOUR FIRE

It's not good enough for me to just tell you *why* it is so important to be enthusiastic and leave out the *how*. The single most important thing I've learned from Anthony Robbins is the importance of questions. Many of my methods for improving creativity have been inspired by his work in this area. The second most important thing I learned from Anthony Robbins is how to control and change your state. In *Unlimited Power*, he provides great insight into how to almost instantly change your mental and emotional state. I took his instruction and tweaked and adapted it into something that has helped my teaching immensely.

The first step to changing your state uses the "act as if" principle. Here is a big secret to enthusiasm that seems so ridiculous you might be tempted to reject it: Unlike passion, enthusiasm can be faked! If you don't believe me, just ask Meg Ryan! (That's a *When Harry Met Sally* reference for those of you out of the loop.) Faking enthusiasm is so easy I can sum it up in two words: *act* enthusiastic! Even if you are only acting at first, an amazing thing happens along the way. You actually start to really feel and become enthusiastic because of your breath pattern and the way you are holding and moving your body.

Do you want to feel powerful? Move your body and breathe in a powerful way. Do you want to be more confident when you are speaking in public? Think about how a confident person moves, sounds, and acts. Do that! Anthony Robbins said, "Acting 'as if' is most effective when you put your physiology in the state you'd be in if you were already effective." There is some truth to the often-disparaged expression, "fake it until you make it." You can instantly change your state by changing your physiology. Robbins explains the change like this: "If you adopt a vital, dynamic, excited physiology, you automatically adopt the same kind of state. The biggest leverage we have in any situation is physiology—because it works so fast, and it works without fail."

I have a ritual for starting class that puts me in the proper state to be effective (discussed in the Rapport chapter). It includes multiple elements of my physiology including posture, breathing, tonality, and movement. It's my way of ensuring I am in my most power-ful state when I present for my class. "Welcome to class, thank you for coming! My name's Dave Burgess and I'll be your host on this

TEACH LIKE A PIRATE!

Learning Extravaganza!" This expression "anchors" me to the state I want to be in. Sometimes, before seminars for example, I use internal dialogue to ready myself to present in a powerful way. I also use music as an anchor. When I hear the pirate music playing in my seminar room it puts me in a place to be ready to dominate. The combination of the music, my internal dialogue, and my changes in body posture and breathing makes me feel absolutely unstoppable.

The second way to change your state is to change what you focus on. You know the feeling of being completely exhausted, when it's all you can do to pry your eyes open and try to keep from nodding off for increasingly longer periods of time. What happens when you remember something critically important that you forgot to do, or the phone rings and someone delivers exciting news? Doesn't your state change within seconds? Suddenly you can't even imagine going to sleep. It would be completely impossible to sleep now because your mind is focused on this new information. That's amazing! You can go from one polar extreme to the other with nothing more than a thought.

As a teacher, your days comprise enough positive and negative experiences to either make you feel energized and amazing or beat down and depressed. What you choose to attend to creates your reality. Some teachers look out over a ninety-nine percent engaged classroom with kids on fire about learning and feel successful. Others choose to focus on the one percent and feel like failures. Make a conscious decision to focus on what empowers you.

I know I simply can't be my most powerful and effective self if I'm not in the right state, so I carefully manage my thoughts to the best of my ability. You wouldn't put trash and destructive chemicals into your car's gas tank, so don't choose to focus on negative and destructive thoughts with your brain. Managing your state is way more important than managing your car, and yet people allow themselves to be dragged down into the muck of negativity. This job is tough enough without having to fight through self-imposed negativity. You'll face plenty of real dragons as an educator; don't create new ones.

When you find yourself in a state that feels less than resourceful, use these two highly effective ways to create a change. Either change your physiology and begin moving in a more powerful and resourceful way, or change the focus of your attention. I highly recommend reviewing the Professional Passion section of the Passion chapter to get some great ideas for what to focus on so you can create a more resourceful and enthusiastic state.

SPREAD THE VIRUS!

By lighting yourself on fire with enthusiasm, you can become a beacon of bliss amidst a bastion of boredom and banality. Your attitude carries with it your single most powerful tool to influence your classroom. Carlos Santana said, "There is nothing more contagious on this planet than enthusiasm. The songs become incidental, what people receive is your joy." As a teacher, I would tweak this to *the lessons become incidental, what people receive is your joy.*

It doesn't particularly matter what the subject is; our mission is to teach in such a way that who we are as human beings has a more powerful and lasting effect on students than what we say. When we model enthusiasm it rubs off on everybody around us; it is absolutely contagious. Be sure to spread it liberally every day, because I guarantee that your students have many people in their lives who are trying to kill their enthusiasm and dampen their spirits. Infect your lessons and everything you do with enthusiasm and then watch it spread.

PART II

CRAFTING
ENGAGING
LESSONS

THE THIRD
CIRCLE

"A good teacher, like a good entertainer, first must hold his audience's attention. Then he can teach his lesson."

HENDRIK JOHN CLARKE

The power of a lesson cannot be maximized without incorporating a masterful presentation. It's like riding a bike with flat tires. You may be doing everything right, but you're working harder than necessary and getting sub-par results. When you have crafted an engaging lesson for your material it is like coasting downhill on a perfectly tuned bicycle with two fully inflated tires. Everything seems easier because the students are drawn into your material as if by some magical or magnetic force.

The *Teach Like a PIRATE* system I presented in Section I lays the foundation for building these magical and magnetic results. All six of those chapters are critically important to effectively reaching and teaching your students. This section focuses on the *how* of creating engaging lessons. It is a "toolbox" of strategies you can draw on to energize your lessons and engage your students. After all, it's one thing to know you *should* engage your students. Actually *being* engaging requires planning, preparation, and presentation.

Take a look at the triple Venn diagram below. The overwhelming majority of professional development workshops focus on the bottom two circles: content and technique/method. Without question, these areas are critical. If you don't have the content element of your lesson in place, you are either just entertaining or babysitting. My assumption is that you are an expert in your subject's content. If not, put this book down and go learn your subject. Come back when you're ready to present a lesson! I'm also making the assumption in this discussion that through your educational program and professional development you have an array of instructional techniques and methods at your disposal. I'm sure you've been to the think-pair-share workshop and the jigsaw session. You've probably learned about scaffolding and SDAIE strategies, attended the literacy training to learn how to build academic vocabulary, and you probably already know the benefits of graphic organizers. Those are *all* good tools and techniques.

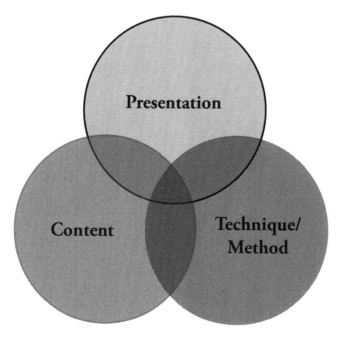

The third circle—presentation—is the critical element most professional development seminars and training materials miss. Nobody is talking to teachers about the third circle, and I'm trying to change that forever. I'm on a one-man mission traveling far and wide to spread the word about the existence and importance of presentation. I have an evangelical zeal for this message.

WELCOME TO THE BBQ

If you come to my house for dinner and you see me out at the BBQ, you have every reason to be excited. You can expect to get a well-prepared and delicious meal. But imagine your surprise if we sat down at the table and I presented you with a plate that was empty with the exception of a completely raw steak. This would be wildly inappropriate!

If I were really going to serve you dinner I'd ask ahead of time if you even like steak. If you don't, I would provide alternatives. If you do like steak, I would season and marinate the meat ahead of time to allow the flavors to soak in. I would preheat the BBQ by turning on the propane (sorry, I know I just lost you coal-only fanatics) and then baste it and turn it until cooked to your specifications. Even after that, I still wouldn't just serve it to you without providing various sides dishes and a beverage to help wash it down. After finishing, I would let you indulge your sweet tooth by providing a scrumptious dessert. That's a meal.

Obviously, you can't serve people raw steak on a plate. However, that's exactly what some educators serve their students every day. Teachers like this walk into class with their raw, unseasoned content, plop it down in front of their kids and say, "Eat it!" They don't bother to provide a side dish, and dessert is way too much trouble. No wonder their students act as if learning is a form of torture that must be endured as they choke down their lessons.

The presentational strategies described in this book that are designed to hook your students and draw them into your lesson are like the seasoning and marinade. You have to prepare these elements ahead of time. You can't just walk into class with a raw, unseasoned steak.

After you've carefully seasoned your lesson and soaked it in student-engagement sauce, you still have to cook it. You have to turn up the heat! In other words, you have to bring energy to your lesson through enthusiasm and showmanship. You have to sell it! You also can't just do it at the beginning of the lesson. For best results, the heat and energy must be maintained. Just like meat has to be turned and basted, you have to continually add engaging twists, turns, and changes of pace throughout the lesson. You must layer your hooks so that engagement doesn't wane. Forty minutes into your class you can't say, "Hey, don't you remember when I said that funny thing forty minutes ago? You should still be paying attention." Layer in as many engaging strategies and techniques as can reasonably fit. I take that back. Layer in those techniques and strategies until it is unreasonable, then scale back later if you have to.

As for the side dishes and dessert, those are the parts of your lesson only the uptight and misguided view as a waste of time. There is no award given to the teacher who fills every class period with bell-to-bell direct instruction. It doesn't matter how much material you teach, it only matters how much is received. By adding in the type of presentational elements featured in this part of the book, you will *not* be wasting precious instructional minutes. Rather, you will be creating a dynamic and well-rounded lesson that is highly engaging, easily memorable, and powerfully impactful.

In addition, no content standard in any class at any level is more important than nurturing and building a love of learning. Designing a class that empowers students to become life-long learners, avid readers, and voracious seekers of knowledge, will have an impact that reverberates for a lifetime and beyond. The point of this section is to help you build presentations in such a way that students will actually want to come to school. When you use the *Teach Like a PIRATE* system and effectively present your material, students will realize education can be fun, entertaining, amazing, and at the same time life-changing.

EVERYTHING IS A CHOICE

Designing lessons is a task filled with an overwhelming number of presentational choices. Everything you do or don't do is a choice. In some of my workshops I perform a mental magic effect with a freely called number from the audience. The whole routine takes about four minutes from start to finish and is usually met with spontaneous applause. In fact, if it isn't met with applause then I did it wrong. Here's the clincher: The whole trick is math. That's right, I perform math in front of the crowd and receive applause. In fact, when I get hired to do a magic show this piece is almost always in my set. Math as a performance art; I get paid to do math!

How is that possible?

Presentation.

After the performance, I go back to the start and show my workshop participants all of the presentational decisions that are a part of those four minutes. There are about ten major presentational decisions—choices—that combine to make an entertaining and effective routine.

If there are ten decisions in a four-minute routine, do the math and figure out how many presentational choices there are in an hour-long lesson. Some choices are major and others are minor, but even the minor decisions, when added up, create impact. Are the lights on when students enter the room? Is there music playing and if so, what? Is there anything written on the board to draw students' attention? Have the desks been rearranged? Do I pass out the handout right away or wait? What do I wear to class to present this lesson? And those are just the presentational decisions that make an impact on a class before the bell rings.

Some of you may be thinking, "I don't make decisions about all of those things for each lesson." Actually, you do. If there is no music playing when students enter your class, it is because you didn't put any on. If you gave no thought to the matter, then what's really going on is that you have abdicated responsibility for that decision. By not consciously controlling the vast array of presentational factors at your disposal, you have diminished your professional power and dampened the potential impact of your lesson.

I know each individual decision, by itself, doesn't seem to matter. The problem, though, is that none of these individual decisions stands alone. Rather, they are woven together into what can be made a beautiful quilt of engagement or an ugly, threadbare blanket of boredom. Determine to intentionally control your environment and all of the presentational elements in play. Everything matters.

TRANSITIONS WILL KILL YOU

One of the ways to tell the difference between a professional magician and an amateur is how they transition from one trick to another. The amateur strings together a series of unrelated or loosely related tricks with awkward pauses and transitions. He does one thing, puts it away, and then searches for the next prop, or tries to think about what he will do next. The pro has a theme that ties his series of effects into an act. One trick naturally flows into another with no awkward pauses or confusion about where he is going next. A professional makes you feel comfortable as an audience because the long, hard work of eliminating awkward moments has created a unifying and congruent experience.

Teaching is exactly the same. After reading this book and practicing the principles, you will have an incredible array of tools to actively engage your class. Don't go to all of the effort to design an amazing and engaging hook for your content only to squander the moment with an ill-timed transition. Your key content—the most important information you are trying to teach—should be delivered at the moment of peak engagement.

Far too many times, teachers capture the attention and engagement of their class and then lose it by adding some unnecessary delay between the hook and the delivery of the content. For example, they tell a powerful story that has the class in the palm of their hand. Then, upon finishing the story, they have the students get a piece of paper out of their notebook before tying it all together with their lesson. They knew that the piece of paper was going to be needed so they should have told the students to get it out before starting the damn story!

Every time you allow or add an unnecessary delay in your presentation you create yet another time that you will have to regain the engagement and momentum you lost. Those two minutes spent putting in and cueing up the video clip matter. Something as simple as waiting for the projector to warm up can be responsible for losing a portion of your audience.

It's not that I'm overly concerned about lost minutes. *Engagement* is the real loss. Every time I lose my students' focus to an unnecessary delay is another time I must go to the hard work of hooking them yet again. It is like a street performer who earns a living by entertaining passersby for tips. The hardest thing to do as a street performer is to build an audience. Therefore, once the audience has been built it is imperative to avoid a break in the performance that would cause people to lose interest and leave.

To keep your students from mentally checking out, try to get all administrative activities out of the way before beginning your presentation. If the students will need any materials (their books, paper, pens, etc.), have them get them out before you start. When you are forced to have a transition, try to make it as quick and seamless as possible. The projector should be warming up while you are giving your high-interest introduction to the video clip. When someone comes into my room with a pass or to take someone out of class, I will either, based on the situation, continue to present my material, or I will banter and interact in an entertaining way with the person who has entered the room so that I maintain engagement. My goal is to avoid coming to a dead stop and losing my audience as a result. That's why, unlike many teachers, I never really get upset at interruptions but choose to position them as more of a game and a challenge. Eliminating and smoothing out transitions may seem like such a small thing to harp on, but the results can be significant.

There is a magical moment I love to create in my classroom. Sometimes it is verbally expressed, other times I can just see it in my students' body language. It is the moment following a highly engaging hook, one that often fills the room with fun and laughter, and all of a sudden they realize, "Hey, he's teaching us!" It's as if they are having such a great time and are so engrossed in the moment that they forget where they are when it dawns on them that they're learning. I picture the toughest and hardest headed students saying, "Dang it! I wasn't going to learn today. He tricked me. That man is sneaky!" I live for that moment.

When I model these techniques in my workshops, I ask the teachers to see if they can find the point at which that moment would happen for a student. Once I teach the concept, most participants can easily and correctly identify it. More importantly, they learn how to design their presentation to include those magical moments. I encourage you to not only master the art of gaining student engagement but also the art of not losing it.

A CRASH
COURSE IN
PRESENTATIONAL
HOOKS

"Do not repeat the means of victory, but respond to form from the inexhaustible."

SUN TZU

This is where the rubber meets the road. In this chapter you'll find one presentational hook after another. If you have ever seen the full-day version of my *Outrageous Teaching: Teach Like a PIRATE* seminar then you know that it is roughly divided into three sections: the *Teach Like a PIRATE* system, the modeling and explanations of multiple presentational hooks, and the collaborative brainstorming session using my *Power Pack* creativity questions. This chapter is a partial combination of the hooks and the creativity questions. It is filled with an unbelievable variety of ideas for drawing students into your content and it also heavily relies on questions that will help you devise ways to incorporate these ideas into your own lessons. If you will take the time to actively consider these questions and intentionally seek ways that they might apply to your class, I think you will be richly rewarded.

When I first decided to get into the professional development business, my number one concern was whether or not I could translate what I do into something that is both teachable and transferable to other educators. Sure, my methods are successful for me, but can I make them accessible to others? Or did they work because of who I am as a person? Today I am thoroughly convinced that any teacher who is willing to put in the time, care, and effort can transform their classroom and their life as an educator using these methods.

Much of your success as an educator has to do with your attitude towards teaching and towards kids. The rest of your success is based on your willingness to relentlessly search for what engages students in the classroom and then having the guts to do it.

When writing this section of my material, I evaluated the presentational hooks I use in my classes and asked myself, "How did I come up with that?" Over and over again, the answer was that I'd asked myself a series of specific types of questions. This chapter includes those exact types of questions. I believe they can lead you to your own creative insights if you will actively and intentionally use them. Because I teach history, many of the examples are history related. Don't be put off by that. The questions and the techniques here are the important factors—not the subject focus. It's not unlike teaching someone to play guitar. First, a student must learn how to hold the instrument, where to put his fingers, and how to strum. Next, he learns basic chord structures. Then, and only then, does the student choose an area focus—classical, jazz, rock 'n' roll. Everyone must learn the basic chords first. This section is teaching chord structure. You will go off and play English, math, science, primary, secondary, and so on. The chord structure remains the same.

I encourage you to use this section of the book as a resource. Return to it any time you need a creative boost for your lessons. I don't know if you have ever seen the MTV show *Pimp My Ride*, but this is the section that will allow you to take run-of-the-mill lessons and "pimp" them for a certain WOW factor. You can work your way through these questions with a particular lesson or unit in mind, or you can just consider your curriculum as a whole and see what sparks a creative idea.

I also recommend that you work collaboratively through this section of the book. Find a colleague with whom you can brainstorm ideas. And, if your first experiences with this brainstorming process are less than you desired, keep at it. The more you engage in these activities, the better you'll get. With practice, you will train your brain to think more creatively. Remember, asking the right questions gives your subconscious mind's search engine a goal. Don't be surprised to find that your best answers come to you well after you've put this book away and have engaged in a completely unrelated activity. When you are engaged in intense creative work, sometimes it isn't until you have let your brain relax and move on that insights occur. I recommend that you have something to write your ideas on as you proceed so that you don't lose them forever.

One final word of instruction for using this section: don't take it too seriously. Be willing to have fun with the process. These questions are in no way meant to be all-inclusive. Feel free to generate your own questions that may better reflect your teaching style. I simply offer these as a starting point and an example of how to become actively engaged in the creative process rather than waiting for that infamous flash of inspiration.

Let's get it on!

"I LIKE TO MOVE IT, MOVE IT"

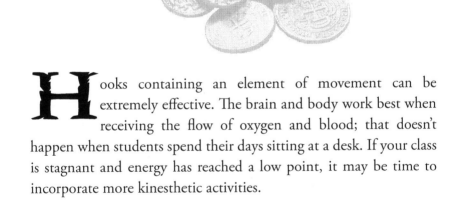

Hooks containing an element of movement can be extremely effective. The brain and body work best when receiving the flow of oxygen and blood; that doesn't happen when students spend their days sitting at a desk. If your class is stagnant and energy has reached a low point, it may be time to incorporate more kinesthetic activities.

THE KINESTHETIC HOOK

 How can I incorporate movement into this lesson?

 Can we throw something, roll something, or catch something inside or outside of class?

 Can we get up and act something out?

Can we incorporate gestures and motions that students could do from their desks?

 Can we turn the room into a giant opinion meter and have students move to one side or the other based on the statement?

 What kind of simulation can we do that would allow them to reenact a part of this lesson?

 Can I change the structure of this lesson from a seated activity to a walk around activity?

 Can I use a game that incorporates movement and action to enhance this lesson?

 How can I guarantee that every student is up and out of their desk at least once during this lesson?

EXAMPLES: My students have collected moon rocks (practice golf balls) that I spread out all over a field behind my class. They have flown like Charles Lindbergh across the Atlantic, roped cattle (or a stool in this case) on a cattle drive, flown paper airplanes during the Berlin Airlift lesson, boarded a Montgomery bus, played intense games of Trench Warfare on the floor behind desks, and fit into a box like Henry "Box" Brown did to mail himself to freedom. They have worked on assembly lines and competed in boot camp obstacle courses. They've even learned to juggle as part of a lesson on the three branches of government.

I promise, you will notice a significant increase in your room's energy when you incorporate movement into your lessons.

IT'S OK TO HAVE FUN

It's never a bad idea to inject some kinesthetic activity into your class, even if the primary goal is to just have some fun. Recently, I presented a lecture about the resistance to slavery and the unique ways slaves sought freedom. After telling them the story of Henry "Box" Brown being mailed to freedom, I challenged my students to try to fit into a box that was smaller in every way than Henry's. We discussed the dimensions and then I let them have at it. I used a large plastic storage bin and they had to get in far enough for me to be able to close the lid. As the day went on things got wilder and wilder! I mentioned to my third period that four students made it in second period, so they proceeded to fit nineteen people in the box. Twenty if you count the campus supervisor who came to deliver a pass and agreed to give it a try. The kids loved it! Fifth period took the challenge and got twenty-two students into the box. The peer pressure to try was intense (but all good-natured). By the time sixth period rolled in, many of the students had heard of the challenge. They stormed into class saying, "Where's the box?" I told them to hold on, they have to learn why there's a box in the first place before getting in it. They set the day's record by fitting twenty-four different students into the box during a class period.

The next day, second period demanded a second chance and fit thirty-one kids in the box. When news of that hit sixth period, they fit ten more students in for a record of thirty-four.

Why am I telling you this?

It's simple. Many teachers would ask the following questions:

- What "standard" is "fitting into a box?"
- Doesn't that waste a lot of time?
- What if nobody wants to try?

Here are some answers:

Sometimes it's OK to do things in class because it increases the fun factor and fosters positive feelings about school. I want students to leave my class with a love of history, a love of learning, and—by the way, also a lot of historical knowledge. This was not the whole period, but a short activity within the context of a lecture. Waste of time? Hardly.

Here's what I saw:

I saw students getting to ponder the experience of Henry and put themselves in his shoes. I saw students excited about the challenge. I had multiple students stop by my room later in the day to check on how the other classes did. I even had students bring in their friends from other classes to try to fit into the box! I saw students cheering and encouraging their peers. I saw students coaching their classmates and giving them tips on technique so that they could also be successful. I saw interactions between students who had never spoken to each other before this activity. There were students who came up to try who had not come to the front of the room for the entire year. I saw a ton of great things come out of what, admittedly, is a pretty silly idea.

I also saw classes full of students who will *never* forget the story of Henry "Box" Brown.

If you are concerned your students wouldn't participate in an activity like this, I have two thoughts. First, you're probably wrong! Second, if you are right then you need to do a better job building rapport and creating an environment where kids feel safe to take a risk.

I love Bill Cosby's line in the theme song to The Fat Albert Show. He says, "This is Bill Cosby coming at you with music and fun and, if you're not careful, you might learn something before we're done." You don't have to apologize for ramping up the entertainment level of your class. In fact, you should apologize to your students if you don't.

It's not necessarily about putting students in the box; it's about thinking outside of the box for creative ideas.

THE PEOPLE PROP HOOK

 How can I make my lesson "play big" by using students as props, inanimate objects, or concepts?

 Can we create a human graph, chart, map, or equation?

 Can students be assigned a specific step in a process or an event and then have to order themselves sequentially?

 Can some students be props and the rest of class "prop movers?"

THE SAFARI HOOK

 How can I get my class outside my four walls for this lesson?

 Where would be the best place(s) on campus to deliver this content?

 Is there an area of the school that serves as the perfect backdrop?

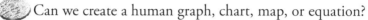 Can I plant key items outside for us to "discover"?

Can we leave campus to go to the ultimate location to teach this material?

Here's the bottom line: Taking your class beyond the classroom walls is a shortcut to engagement because it is so novel. Of course, it comes with challenges. But I didn't say any of this would be easy.

Examples: Each year I take my students on the Trail of Tears walk. It is a forty-minute walk along a trail that goes around some of the outer fields of the campus. I arrive way before school starts and set up the trail with all sorts of props and scenes. During the class period, we walk together as a group. When we come upon one of the areas set up with props, the whole class pulls in tight so they can hear the lecture. What better way to teach about the Trail of Tears than to actually walk along a trail?

I have also taken classes outside to reenact battles, march and train like soldiers, and roast marshmallows. You have freedom to do all sorts of activities outside the confines of your classroom, so get outside!

LONG LIVE
THE ARTS

*"Every child is an artist. The problem is how
to remain an artist once he grows up."*

PABLO PICASSO

Music and art can be incredibly powerful ways to engage
our students and enhance our lessons. We have unbelievably talented kids sitting in front of us and many
are starving for the opportunity
to display their creativity. We
should do everything we can to
provide them the opportunity
to hone their artistic skills and
create. Even our students who
consider themselves inartistic
can and will benefit from the
chance to explore and create.

*"It is the supreme art of the
teacher to awaken joy in creative
expression and knowledge."*

ALBERT EINSTEIN

THE PICASSO HOOK

 How can I incorporate art into this lesson?

 What can my students draw or make that would help them understand and retain this information?

 Can they make some kind of non-linguistic representation of the material? (A photography project or 3-D art, for example.)

 Can they create visuals of key information as a way to review for the upcoming test?

 Can they design word pictures in which the way the word is written reveals its definition?

 Can I create an art-based option that students could choose instead of another assignment?

Examples: After finishing a unit, I often provide a day for students to get into collaborative groups and create non-linguistic representations of the material. For example, I may ask them to create a visual depicting an event or concept. It can be a literal interpretation or a symbolic representation; I encourage my students to be as creative as possible. To decide how they'll create their drawing, they must review and process the content together. The Picasso Hook allows students to review and recall material from the lecture in a different way. The simple fact that they are interacting with the concepts again is beneficial. Processing the material collaboratively, visually, and artistically also aids in retention. Not only do they participate in a decision-making process about what to draw, they are likely to remember the picture even if they forget the lecture. Finally, let's not forget the added benefit of allowing students to flex and train their creative muscles.

I like to provide project opportunities that allow students to use their artistic talents whenever possible. For example, I have had students design the signs that decorate my room for the sixties party. I have had geography students write their vocabulary word in a way that the shape or organization of the letters serve as a visual definition. The word peninsula, for instance, should be written so that it looks like a peninsula.

In my opinion, it is ideal to give students the option of replacing a standard assignment with one that allows them to use their creative spirit and skills. You might be truly amazed at the results. You don't even have to design and define the project; let them design and define it and then get approval. I believe you will find that some of your students who seem disengaged will blossom and come alive when they are free to use their creativity.

THE MOZART HOOK

 How can I use music to aid my presentation?

 What would be the perfect song or type of music to create the right mood and proper atmosphere?

 What songs have lyrics that relate to this lesson?

 If I don't know, can I ask my students to find examples from their music that relate to this topic?

 How can I most effectively use music as they enter the room?

 How can I improve the start of my lesson with the perfect song selection?

What should we listen to while students are working independently or collaboratively?

 Can I use music to make my transitions smoother and more engaging?

 How can I use music to wrap up my lesson and send them out into the world in a positive and upbeat mood?

 Can I offer an alternative project that would allow my students with musical talents to be creative?

 Can I allow students to create songs/raps that demonstrate their understanding of the content as an alternative to essays and standard reports?

 Can students change the lyrics to popular songs to reflect course content? (Think "Weird" Al Yankovic.)

Music is an unbelievable state and mood changer. It has the ability to touch our soul like few other mediums. If you want to change the atmosphere in the classroom, sometimes all that is required is a change (or addition) of song. The right selection can bring a serious and meditative tone to the class, or create a rowdy and rambunctious energy fest.

Music instantly transports us back to the past. I still remember the feelings that shot through me when Trevor Hoffman walked to the mound at a Padres game in the ninth inning to try for a save. The scoreboard went dark and the bells started ringing. The sound sent chills through the entire stadium. It was powerful, and the sound helped make the scene *memorable*.

Examples: Just like radio stations play bumper music coming in and out of breaks; I play music during passing periods as students are leaving and entering the room. I use songs with lyrics that relate to my topics such as Public Enemy's, *Can't Truss It* for my lesson on the Middle Passage and a short section of Paris' *Escape From Babylon* when discussing the Ten-Point Program of the Black Panthers. I use era and mood appropriate music for my Speakeasy simulation and discuss jazz in relationship to the Harlem Renaissance. We learn all about the history of rock 'n' roll when we study the fifties, including genres of music that influenced its development and early pioneers of the style. It is, of course, easy and necessary to show how the music of the sixties reflected, and in some ways even shaped, the attitudes and events of that tumultuous decade. I use scary, mood altering music to build a creepy atmosphere for my Salem Witchcraft Trial experience. My Lunar Landing Lesson heavily relies on Pink Floyd's *Dark Side of the Moon* album to create just the right atmosphere. The list could go on and on but suffice it to say that music is too powerful a force to ignore in your classroom. Whether you use it to create a mood or tie it into your curriculum, music is an element of presentational power that can help you transform your class. Because it is so powerful, I am constantly looking for opportunities for my students to use their musical prowess in my class. This helps to reinforce the value I place on their unique talents and allows them additional chances to see school as a place that encourages rather than stifles creativity.

THE DANCE AND DRAMA HOOK

 Can I provide the opportunity for my students to do skits or appear in videos related to what we are learning?

 Can they learn and perform a relevant dance?

Can some of the students teach a dance to the class?

 Can they impersonate key people from history in a panel discussion or interview format?

 Can they reenact historical events?

 Can they write a script and create a video to play for the class?

The drama and dance hook allows you to incorporate a kinesthetic element into your class, as well as provide a creative outlet for your students. You can quickly determine which students excel at this type of activity and, interestingly enough, it is often students who struggle with other classroom activities. Providing variety in the way students can access your curriculum and display their knowledge of it ensures that you are reaching everyone.

EXAMPLES: During a unit on the twenties, I have had students make Charleston dance videos. They've also made videos of the fad dances when we study the fifties. Skits, simulations, and reenactments are too many to name and are scheduled throughout the year.

THE CRAFT STORE HOOK

 How can I incorporate a craft into this lesson?

 What can my students make that relates to this material?

 Is there an origami fold that I can teach to the class for this content?

Can I provide some basic supplies such as craft sticks, pipe cleaners, and duct tape, give them an open-ended creative project, and turn them loose?

 Could there be craft skills my students already possess that could enhance my curriculum and simultaneously allow them the chance to be an expert for a day?

EXAMPLES: I teach how to fold an origami crane in my lesson about the aftermath of the atomic bombings of Hiroshima and Nagasaki. See the "Don't Let Critics Steal Your Soul" story on page 161 for more on this lesson's controversial focus.

On the day we reenact Lindbergh's flight, students construct their own flight goggles using duct tape, craft sticks, and pipe cleaners. They have complete creative license to make the goggles any way they want, and they consistently come up with absolutely amazing designs. I know many students who have kept their flight goggles for years after they have left my class.

To encourage students to use their ingenuity, I put out random craft supplies and have them design and make inventions that would be helpful for various historical periods. For example, they can demonstrate that they understand the difficulties and challenges faced by the various groups during westward expansion (like cowboys, mountain men, Native Americans, Gold Rush miners, Lewis and Clark, homesteaders, outlaws) by making something that would have eased their burden. When conducted as a group project, the discussion that takes place about what problem to solve and how to solve it helps drive home the lesson.

WHAT'S IN IT FOR ME?

"A teacher who is attempting to teach without inspiring the pupil to learn is hammering on a cold iron."

HORACE MANN

It's human nature to ask (or at least think), *What's in it for me?* We all want to know how current events might have an impact on our lives. Advertisers and copywriters have long known that persuasive copy must answer this essential question. People are rarely impressed by the features of a product; it's the benefits the features provide that really matter. The next few hooks will help you design lessons with that crucial question in mind.

THE STUDENT HOBBY HOOK

 How can I incorporate the hobbies and outside interests of my students into this material?

 Do I even know the hobbies and outside interests of my students and, if not, how can I find out?

How can I harness the power of connecting my content to what students are *already* interested in?

THE REAL-WORLD APPLICATION HOOK

 How can I show my students why learning this content is important in the real world?

 How will they possibly apply this in their life?

 Can we increase motivation and engagement by offering reasons to learn that go beyond "because it's on the test?"

 Can they create something "real" that will be more than a classroom project but actually allow them to interact with the world in an authentic way?

THE LIFE-CHANGING LESSON HOOK

 How can I use this lesson to deliver an inspirational message?

 What type of life-changing lesson can be incorporated into the content?

 What type of essential questions can I ask that allow students the opportunity for personal reflection and growth?

THE STUDENT-DIRECTED HOOK

 How can I provide opportunities for autonomy and choice in this unit/lesson?

Can I allow student interest to dictate our direction and learning while still covering what we need to address?

How can I release some of my control and provide students the chance to be the experts and directors of this subject?

The "unconference" and "edcamp" movements are examples of what can happen when teachers are allowed to direct their own professional development experience. Allowing students to experience similar freedom might be liberating and fulfilling for the more self-directed learners. And for those who rely on step-by-step direction, that sort of freedom is an opportunity for growth. In his incredible book, *Drive: The Surprising Truth About What Motivates Us*, Daniel Pink posits that one of three key elements for motivating people is to provide a high level of autonomy. How are you consistently providing choice and autonomy in your classroom?

THE OPPORTUNISTIC HOOK

 What current events are related to this lesson?

 Is there a hot topic in the news or on campus that I can use to capture student interest?

 What aspect of current pop culture can I tie into this material?

 In what ways can I incorporate currently popular trends, fads, TV shows, and movies in order to make this relevant and engaging for my class?

 Can I put intriguing images of current events on the walls with QR codes underneath that link to more information?

Associating your curriculum with current events not only increases engagement because it shows relevance, it also helps students become more globally aware and connected. Teaching students how to see events from different perspectives and analyze bias in coverage is also fantastic for teaching media literacy and critical thinking.

ALL THE WORLD IS A STAGE

Controlling the physical space of my room is one of my secret weapons. I am the director, producer, stage manager, and lead actor for the one hundred eighty different performances that will take place in and around my room. It is my stage, and I honor and value it as such. Anything I can do to manipulate and control the environment is fair game. This is a tough business; I'm more than willing to take advantage of and influence everything around me to increase my students' chances of success.

THE INTERIOR DESIGN HOOK

 How can I transform my room to create the ultimate atmosphere for this lesson?

 Can I change the lighting for mood?

Can I block out all light and just use accent lights to emphasize certain things?

 Can I cover or decorate the walls, the ceiling, or the floor?

 Can I change the entrance so no one can see into class?

 How can I rearrange the desks for this lesson to be most effective?

 Can I create more space by removing desks?

 Can I add partitions to break the room into areas or to create maze-like corridors?

 If I were throwing a theme party at my house for this subject, what would I do?

If a theme park were opening up a new attraction based on my lesson, what would it include?

I often change the whole look of my classroom for a single lesson. One of the ways I do this is by using what I call the blank slate theory. Instead of constantly changing bulletin boards and walls for each unit or season, I tend to have a basic look for my class. On special days I create a blank canvas by completely covering every wall with enormous rolls of black plastic sheeting. The rolls are ten feet high and twenty-five feet long, so it doesn't take many to get the job done. Then I can add what I want as decorations on top of the black background. The sheeting also cuts out all light from the windows and allows me to use accent lights to create any type of mood I want. The different look and feel of my room often shocks students when they walk in, especially when I set the scene by hanging sheets at the entryway to obscure the room from view. The effect of the ceiling-to-floor drape makes students feel as if they're entering the room through a curtain. I have also used sheets to create hallways and separate chambers inside the main room.

For lessons that require additional space, I remove desks from the room and put them in my office or outside the door. Desks can also be used as props to suit the lesson. For example, I've configured desks for use in assembly lines, as a bus for the Montgomery Bus Boycotts, or in separate construction groups for building suburban houses.

EXAMPLES: I create a very dark and creepy feel for my room for the Salem Witchcraft Trials. In fact, between the darkness of the transformed room, the scary music, and me dressed as a witch, it is not unusual for a few students to be a little scared and creeped out.

For my Lunar Landing Lesson I remove every trace of light from the room. I clear out about eighty percent of the desks to allow students to lie on the floor with their backpacks under their head. They enter a room that is dimly lit with accent lights. Pink Floyd music plays in the background. The period consists of a short lecture from me about landing on the moon and exactly how unbelievably incredible such a feat was for 1969. I also wrap in a couple life-changing lessons about the power of possibility and the paradigm shift that can occur from seeing Earth from outer space. When you realize we are living on a blue ball hurdling through an expansive universe, most of our worries, stresses, and obsessions with petty differences suddenly seem ridiculous. Next we watch a space video synced to Pink Floyd's *Dark Side of the Moon*. Finally, I turn off the accent lights and put on a multicolor laser show on the ceiling complete with music. It is an amazing day that students talk about for years afterwards. It has content standards covered, life-changing lessons, and an unbelievable experience all rolled into one period.

Those student-created posters I mentioned in The Picasso Hook section help transform my class for the sixties party which culminates our study of that decade. For my Red Scare lesson, the entire room is covered in red sheeting (I use red plastic table covers from a party supply store). My Speakeasy Lesson is another complete room make-over which includes darkness, accent lights, music, a bar area, and multiple gaming tables. One of the benefits of using the blank-slate theory for my room is that when the lesson is done, you just remove the coverings and your normal wall decorations and bulletin boards are still there.

THE BOARD MESSAGE HOOK

 What can I write on my board or have projected on my screen that will immediately spark curiosity and interest as the students enter my room?

 What type of message will create a buzz and provoke students to point it out and begin to talk to each other about it before the bell even rings?

 What can I write that will be intriguing and mysterious and compel students to approach me and ask questions before we get started?

 Can I just put a QR code on the board or screen and see what happens?

 Can I have an intriguing image projected that will eventually tie into my content?

Actively engaging students *before* the class period even starts makes for an interesting period. An intriguing board message or image can create a scenario where students are curious about the content and primed to listen. Isn't that what you want? My goal is to make the message something that has kids talking and buzzing even before the bell rings. I love it when it compels them to approach me with a question.

Messages work on adult audiences, too. When I am conducting the full PIRATE presentation at a teaching seminar, I place a sign at the front of the room before the session starts that reads,

THE #1 TOP SECRET WAY TO BECOME A BETTER LOVER!!

People can't help but to be curious; it creates a buzz and lifts the energy level in the room before I even start talking. I have seen women take pictures of the sign and send it to their husbands with a "look what I'm learning today" text. I have been asked many times to pose with teachers in front of the sign after the presentation. The right board message works!

THE COSTUME HOOK

 What can I wear as an outfit or costume for this lesson?

 Is there an existing character that I can impersonate?

Can I create a character that is relevant to this lesson?

 Can I invent a superhero or super villain for this subject?

What accessory (something as small as a hat or glasses) can I wear to enhance my presentation?

In my class, when I'm dressed in costume I call it a guest-speaker day. My students know not to miss days when a "guest speaker" is on the schedule. If I'm well-known on my campus for one thing, this is it. Here is a partial list of my characters:

Salem Witch
Supreme Court Justice
Sherlock Holmes (seeking historical clues)
Mountain Man
Cowboy
Suffragette
Prohibition-era Gangster
Priest
Rosie the Riveter
50s Teenage Girl in a Poodle Skirt
The Red Scare Super Villain
The 10-Man (superhero that teaches the first ten amendments)
Hippie
Trail Guide

Whew!

I also rarely give a professional-development workshop or keynote speech without creating a character. Obviously, I dress as a pirate, but I've also shown up as BTSA Man (Beginning Teacher Support and Assessment), ESLR Man (Expected School-wide Learning Results), a doctor for my Educational E.R. workshop, and as a construction worker for my Building a Better Teacher keynote. Ramping up the entertainment value of presentations leads to greater engagement and costumes and characters are techniques I often employ.

If you're concerned about looking foolish in front of your students, the best advice I can offer is *get over it*. I know I look outrageous and that people are going to gawk and laugh at me, and I'm OK with that. If you're going to use the Costume Hook, you have to be comfortable in your own skin, and you definitely have to *own* whatever persona you are taking on that day. That said, you don't have to not be self-conscious, you just have to, as Anthony Robbins says, "act as if" you aren't self-conscious. I know that of all of these techniques, this is one I most often have people, especially men, say they wouldn't be able to pull off, but you won't know unless you try it.

THE PROPS HOOK

 What physical item can I bring in to add to my presentation?

 What image can I show?

Instead of just talking about a book, can I bring it?

 Instead of just mentioning a person, can I show their picture?

What can I bring that students could actually hold in their hands and pass up and down the aisles?

I'm a big believer in props. I use a slew of them in my workshops. In fact, they take up most of my luggage space and have led to some interesting moments at airport security. Props are as critical to my workshop and seminar presentations as they are in the classroom. It is much more effective to talk about the coin made to commemorate Susan B. Anthony *and* to pull it out, show it, and pass it around. When we are talking about a book, I like to have it or at least an image of it. It's way better to actually have a Minie ball than to simply talk about Civil War bullets.

For those of you who lecture using PowerPoint, Prezi, Keynote, or other onscreen presentations, you can substitute images for props. Cut way down on your text and bullet points and incorporate more images. Bullet points and text-heavy slides put your students to sleep! You'll have more luck engaging them using plentiful high-interest pictures.

THE INVOLVED AUDIENCE HOOK

 How can I consistently keep the audience feeling involved?

 Can I cue them to make certain motions or sounds at key points?

 Can I incorporate call and response into this lesson?

 Can I, unknown to their classmates, cue certain students to play a pre-arranged role?

Can I bring students to the front of the room as volunteers?

Anything that makes students feel like they are actually part of the show, not just spectators, is a good thing. For example, I incorporate call and response when teaching the Bill of Rights. Sometimes I use a tactic I call Choreographed Chaos, in which I pre-arrange for a student or group of students to play a role in my lesson. To the rest of the class it seems strange and chaotic but it has been completely choreographed. It is like a flash mob but on a smaller scale and in a classroom. What makes a flash mob fun is that not everyone is in on it. Seeing the reactions of other people to the pre-arranged events is what makes Choreographed Chaos fun. I will often use my class clowns as the actors in my Choreographed Chaos segments. They want to get attention and interject themselves into your lesson anyway, so why not have it be on your terms and in a way that serves your message?

THE MYSTERY BAG HOOK

 How can I gain engagement by openly hiding something from the class?

Can I have a closed box or a package on the front stand?

 How can I build up the suspense of the unveiling?

 Can I cut a hole into a box so that students reach inside and feel the contents but not see?

 Can I give hints and open the floor for guesses?

 What can I put into the mystery box or bag that would tie to my lesson?

 After displaying the item, how can I get students to try to figure out the relationship between it and the lesson?

A famous moment in my workshop has to do with what I pull out of a bag while demonstrating this hook. We have a natural curiosity about that which we cannot see. It kills us to know something is being kept from us. This is the principle on which Christmas presents and birthday presents work. What is the distinguishing feature of a present that makes it intriguing and engaging? It's wrapped! You can't see it and you want to know what it is. The first thing we do is pick it up and see how heavy it is. Then we may shake it. If all of our presents were unwrapped, receiving them wouldn't be such a big deal.

We can use this universally engaging principle in our class. Trust me, if your students see a wrapped package at the front of the room when they come in, you will be fielding a ton of questions. If you can tie the moment of peak engagement, which is the unveiling of the contents, to your curriculum…you have a golden moment.

STAND AND DELIVER

Do you consider yourself a public speaker? When asked this question, most teachers emphatically respond, "No!" Some even claim that the thought of speaking in front of crowds terrifies them. I find this fascinating because in a very real sense *all* teachers are full-time professional speakers. In fact, I would venture to guess many teachers do more public speaking in their classroom than the vast majority of speakers do on the circuit. You are a public speaker, own it and be intentional about honing your skills of engagement. Here are six hooks that can lead to a better classroom performance.

THE STORYTELLING HOOK

 What captivating story can I tell that would draw students into this lesson?

 Can I create a high-interest story to fit the lesson?

 What techniques of the master storytellers, such as dramatic build, can I use to enhance this presentation?

 How would speaking in character, using accents, changing intonations, and varying volume for effect (even whispering) have an impact on the class?

 How can I use facial expressions, dramatic pauses, and gestures to improve the power of my lecture?

> *"The universe is made of stories, not of atoms."*
>
> MURIEL RUKEYSER

I love to watch great storytellers do their thing. I try to learn as much as I can from the experts who so powerfully and effectively deliver their messages. But the goal isn't just to learn. I consciously work to apply and adapt their techniques to my own work. Where can I create interest? How can I capture my students' attention? Where can I add punch to the story?

An effectively told story might become the most powerful thing you do in front of any audience. It's no wonder the most persuasive and impactful people in human history have used stories as their primary mode of instruction. Whether to lead great armies, great nations, or great religions, they've used stories for one reason: they work.

THE SWIMMING WITH THE SHARKS HOOK

 How can I enter the audience and break down the barrier between teacher and class?

 Can I participate in the activity?

 Can I storm up and down the rows and use the whole room as my platform?

 Can I enter the physical space of key areas in the room where attention is waning?

Is there a different place, or multiple places, that I can present from for the sake of novelty?

A silent agreement exists between many teachers and their classes. Content is presented from the front middle (up here) and received from the rows or tables (out there). Breaking down this invisible wall between teacher and class when you are presenting can increase engagement simply due to its novelty. The worst-case scenario for me when I present is a fixed microphone. In fact, I tell the planners that it is untenable. Next worse is a limited corded microphone. I love to be able to move back and forth and into the audience when presenting. When presenters are kinesthetically active the audience responds with increased energy. When presenters and teachers stand in one spot for an hour, their audience members tend to fall asleep. Don't get stuck presenting every lesson from the same spot.

THE TABOO HOOK

 How can I use the fact that students are fascinated by that which is taboo and forbidden?

 How can I position my topic so that it seems like a little-known secret?

 How can I take advantage of the fact that students (and adults!) are intrigued by things they aren't supposed to hear?

Can I position my topic as if it is illicit, even though it isn't?

When someone sits at the next table, don't you want to know what they're talking about? Sure you do! It's human nature. We all want to be "in the know." Knowing that somebody has a secret can eat us up inside until we find out. Topics that are taboo, forbidden, or seemingly illicit, make us curious. (The success of *50 Shades of Grey* comes to mind.) I often position my content as if it is little known, a secret, or just recently discovered. I also don't mind positioning it as possibly inappropriate. What I actually say will not be, but it is positioned as such. The "Better Lover" sign mentioned earlier is an example. Nothing that I tell teachers at my workshops is illicit, but that sign positions the content as if it might be. The intended effect is to generate interest and create a buzz—and it works! Obviously, you need to adjust your taboo hook for the age and maturity of your students, but even a kindergartener will be drawn in by the possibility of learning a secret or something their

> *"A story is told as much by silence as by speech."*
>
> SUSAN GRIFFIN

friends or parents don't know. Advertisers routinely use the "taboo hook" to sell billions of dollars of products. I use it to sell education.

THE MIME HOOK

 How can I use the mesmerizing power of silence to spark interest and engage?

 Can I use nothing but written messages to deliver my lesson or opening hook?

 Can I use mime techniques and gestures to get my point across?

 Can I incorporate charades and/or Pictionary-type activities?

 Can students be asked to get their messages across without words, as well?

THE TEASER HOOK

 How can I spark interest in this lesson by promoting it ahead of time?

 What can I do to create a positive expectancy in advance?

 What aspect of this lesson can I tease beforehand to provoke curiosity?

 If I were creating a movie trailer or preview for this lesson, what would it include?

 If I were planning a marketing promotion for this lesson what would I do and when would I begin?

I firmly believe you should promote your lessons ahead of time. I want to do everything in my power to build a positive sense of expectancy about my class. "Don't miss tomorrow, there is going to be an unbelievably strange opening to class." "There is a guest speaker (me in costume) coming on Friday and I've got one word—tights!" Students simply don't miss the days I promote and they have even forced parents to switch appointment times or bring them back to school afterwards. I start promoting and selling the Lunar Landing Lesson and the sixties party during the first week of school—and they don't happen until deep into second semester. I also use a Facebook fan page to promote my lessons and build up high expectations and eager anticipation. The movie industry makes trailers because they work; they make you want to see the movie. I want people to *want* to see my lesson. Think about it. When performers and speakers have great introductions, it instantly builds credibility and positive expectations even before they hit the stage. It becomes a self-fulfilling prophecy, if people think something is going to be great they are more likely to experience it as such. The same approach can work in your class for your lessons. *Promote*, *market*, and *sell* are three business practices that belong in the classroom.

THE BACKWARDS HOOK

 How can I gain an advantage or increase interest by presenting this material out of sequence?

 Can I tell them the end of the story and let them figure out and discover the beginning and middle?

 Can I show them an end product that will make them want to learn the skills to get there?

Perhaps the best way to explain the Backwards Hook is by equating it to a TV show like *CSI*. Each episode starts with a dead body and a crime scene. The rest of the show is spent figuring out how it got there. The incredible Ken Burns documentary, *The Civil War*, starts by showing pictures of the aftermath of the war. He pans across destroyed cities and battlefields strewn with dead soldiers while the narrator gives unfathomable statistics of how many died. You're left with this overwhelming feeling of how could this have happened in America. After those high-impact scenes, historians come on and explain why this war is so important to American history. By starting with the end, Burns sets the stage and then goes all the way back to the beginning to tell the long story of how America got to that dreadful end. That is the backwards hook.

ADVANCED TACTICS

The following three hooks can really ramp up the engagement level of your class—*if* properly applied.

THE MISSION IMPOSSIBLE HOOK

 How can I design my lesson so that students are trying to unravel and solve a mystery?

 How can I incorporate clues that can only be decoded by learning or researching the relevant subject? (Think *The Da Vinci Code* and *National Treasure.*)

 Can they be provided a treasure map or sent on a scavenger hunt through your content?

What type of entertaining plot can I use as an overlay or backdrop for this unit?

 What fictitious character or role can they play?

 What crisis must they prevent?

 Can I change this from a standard assignment to a daring and impossible mission?

THE REALITY TV HOOK

 How can I design my lesson to take advantage of the popularity of reality TV?

 Can I create a *Survivor*-style challenge and divide the class into tribes?

Can this be configured as an *Amazing Race* partner lesson?

How can I incorporate a *Fear Factor* type of challenge?

A perfect example of incorporating a *Fear Factor* type challenge comes from my colleague Reuben Hoffman. When discussing the differences in cultural norms around the world, he brings in a wild variety of food from different countries. Many of the kids are terrified to try some of the stranger (to them, anyway) types of food. Volunteers come up and spin a wheel and they have to eat what it lands on. They learn about cultural norms, try some exotic foods, and have an absolute blast during this high-interest lesson.

THE TECHNO WHIZ HOOK

 How can I tap into the technological prowess of my students?

 Can I give my students the option to create projects and turn in assignments digitally?

> *"Any sufficiently advanced technology is indistinguishable from magic."*
> ARTHUR C. CLARKE

 Can I create a paperless lesson, unit, or class?

 How can this lesson benefit from the fact that many students have more computing power in their pockets and backpacks than I have in my class or lab?

 How can I take advantage of the fact that most phones now have camera, video, and Internet capability?

 How can I leverage the power of social media to empower my students to engage in their education beyond the standard school day?

 How can technology be used to bridge gaps between school and the real world?

 How can technology help to connect my students to people from all over the world and help them gain a global perspective?

 How can I utilize the latest apps to create more powerful and interactive presentations? (I intentionally refrained from listing specific programs, apps, or hardware because technology changes so fast, my recommendations would probably be outdated by the time you read this.)

"Don't fight forces; use them."
R. BUCKMINSTER FULLER

The technological revolution is not going to go away. Students are used to the ability to connect to each other and have access to information at all times. We can either fight against this irrepressible force, or we can choose to use it. If you are committed to the *Teach Like a PIRATE* system, you should always be willing to adapt to the changing atmospheric conditions. Our aim is to chart a new course through the educational seas and to maximize the resources at our disposal. Use technology as a teaching tool. Harness your students' knowledge of and familiarity with this tool to help them succeed. When used correctly, technology can enhance the effectiveness of your lesson, increase engagement, and even strengthen the relationships between the humans that comprise your class.

THE POWER OF LIVE!

I saw Juan Tamariz, one of the greatest magicians in the world, perform card magic at the 2010 Magic Con conference. I had seen him perform on video many times but it paled in comparison to seeing him live. It was an amazing and transformative experience. On the first night he simply sat in a chair at a small table in the hotel hallway and proceeded to hold court in front of a huge group of magicians who crowded and surrounded the table at least ten rows deep. I saw an entire audience of well-posted, knowledgeable magicians with their jaws on the floor and in a complete state of astonishment. He completely devastated the crowd. He took us on an emotional rollercoaster ride and weaved a masterful performance that was not just amazing and entertaining, but also inspiring and uplifting. It was a once in a lifetime moment. Why was it so powerful? It was LIVE! He was able to play off of the crowd, improvise, shift and change directions, and build his effects into emotional climaxes. He wasn't just manipulating playing cards... he was manipulating people. Furthermore, the presentation was powerful because it was a shared experience. The group dynamic helped create an electric vibe. That exact moment can never be duplicated. If there was a video of the performance you might as well burn it. Like so many things in life, it was one of those "you had to be there" moments.

Compare listening to music in your car to attending a live concert. It is undeniably and qualitatively different. What if you were the only person there? That would also be qualitatively different because a large part of the magic of a live concert is the shared experience and feeling of community. Ask a Deadhead if the CD of the show is the same as being there. It's different.

Try this: Go to YouTube and watch someone walking on the beach. Then go to the beach and feel the waves wash over your feet and the sand between your toes. Punch "Grand Canyon" into Google images and take a look. Then go stand on the edge and gaze down. Let's assume you can't swim. Go do a month's worth of online research and read and watch everything you can about how to swim. Now go jump in the deep end of the pool. I'm guessing thirty minutes with a live instructor in the water would have served you better than all that online research.

Nothing is more powerful than a master teacher standing before a class of students orchestrating the learning experience. The teacher can instantly shift directions after intuitively sensing a lack of under-standing or engagement. He or she can provide instantaneous feedback, read body language, facial expressions and vocal intonation. The teacher is able to lead discussions, bring enthusiasm, and inject emotion and intensity at just the right time. A masterful teacher can determine when it is appro-priate to temporarily drop the lesson altogether in order to capture that elusive teachable moment that might be far more significant than the content standard on the board.

Every year—and even every period—will be a little different because of the different students that make up the community of the classroom. A group of people sharing a common experience and inter-acting in a face-to-face environment is not outdated or obsolete. It is the handwritten thank you note in a world of email, tweets, and texts. It still works.

Technology, as one of a multitude of tools in the hands of an expert educator, can be undeniably powerful. However, technology as a replacement for live interaction between teachers and students concerns me. Sure, I know some students are bored and disengaged in their traditional classes but that sounds like an argument for better professional development and training for teachers, not for sticking kids in front of a computer screen all day. I'm just not ready to jump completely onto the online learning bandwagon quite yet. I know the horse might be out of the barn, but I have concerns that the pendulum might be swinging too far towards a love affair with technology just for the sake of technology. Using it in new and creative ways is a natural, positive progression that should be encouraged. But I fear many have become almost cult-like in their allegiance to it.

I have great hopes for the educational technology revolution that is sweeping the world right now but its best use is to augment and increase the effectiveness of teachers, not replace them. I still believe in the "POWER OF LIVE!"

AROUND THE EDGES

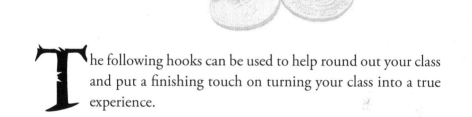

The following hooks can be used to help round out your class and put a finishing touch on turning your class into a true experience.

THE CONTEST HOOK

 How can I include a contest in this lesson to build excitement and motivation?

 What type of review game can I design to ramp up the entertainment level of my class?

 What kind of in-class challenge can I create that would take advantage of their competitive instinct?

Can I be a part of the challenge or contest?

Students love a contest or a challenge too much to ignore this as a tool of engagement. I especially like to design unusual and fun review games before we take tests because it's hard for even the toughest student to ignore the challenge. For example, we play an incredible game of trench warfare before testing on WWI. Students get down on the floor in opposing trenches and try to "kill" each other with a "bomb." The only way your side gets to throw a bomb, though, is to answer a review question correctly. We have a totally effective test review and play an unbelievably fun game at the same time. I also use a battleship review game where the room is divided into two teams and, after getting a question right; they may take a shot at the other team's grid. If one team calls out "B-three" and the other team has a student's name written in that spot, they're dead. Here's a tip: To have multiple winners and more fun throughout the game, offer additional ways to win other than just surviving. For example, those who give the best dramatic death performance or deliver the best dying words can also get bragging rights as Battleship Winners in my class. Again, we are reviewing content but having a blast doing it.

THE MAGIC AND THE AMAZING HOOK

 What amazing principle can I demonstrate as part of this lesson?

 Is there a magical effect that could help to deliver this message?

 Can I teach my students an amazing skill that they will go home and show others?

I'm constantly on the prowl for magical and amazing principles. I write them down in a notebook and then try to brainstorm ways to incorporate them in my class. I love this hook so much that I teach a breakout session workshop explaining how to use these magical and amazing ideas in the classroom. Some effects break the ice, and others are integral to the lessons and are fully routined to teach my content standards. In the workshop, we discuss how to use the creative process to generate ideas for specific curriculum.

THE CHEF HOOK

 How can I enhance this lesson by adding food or drinks?

 Can I cook something for the class?

 What type of food would be a perfect match for this lesson?

 How can I use food or drinks to demonstrate a point, serve as an incentive, or just help create a positive atmosphere for a special lesson?

I have a full-service, non-alcoholic bar on the day of my speakeasy. *The Jungle*, by Upton Sinclair, includes a disgusting section about the meat-packing industry and how sausage was made at the turn of the century. After reading it, I tell them I have prepared sausage to be historically accurate, and then proceed to bring it out for them to eat. The whole time I'm asking if they taste rat or rat dung. This is not only fun, but serves as an experience to help them remember the lesson of the day about progressive reforms and muckrakers. When we learn about the mountain men and tell tall tales, we cook s'mores. When learning about fear of the atomic bomb in the fifties, I pass out Atomic Fireball candy.

I'm always looking for ways to make my class memorable and enjoyable. Using food and drinks from time to time is one of my tactics.

THE MNEMONIC HOOK

 Are there key bits of information I want my students to know cold?

 Is there a pattern to point out?

 Can the point of the lesson be tied to previous knowledge?

 Does a mnemonic exist for the material?

 Can I design my own mnemonic to help them remember this material?

 Can the students create their own mnemonic?

 How can I embed a mnemonic theme throughout my presentation to aid retention?

I have long been fascinated with memory. I can remember being blown away by Harry Lorayne's *The Memory Book*. Since reading it, I have incorporated memory demonstrations, such as memorizing an entire *Time* magazine, into many of my magic performances. I extensively used mnemonics to retain content while in college and now try to incorporate as many mnemonics as I can to help my students. An example would be a mnemonic I created to teach the Bill of Rights. Using the six letters of the word PIRATE as the organizational principle for my seminar and book is an example of designing a presentation with an imbedded mnemonic overlay to aid retention.

We owe it to students to help them not only be engaged by our content, but to retain it, as well.

THE EXTRA-CREDIT CHALLENGE HOOK

 What high-interest and motivating challenges can I create that relate to this unit?

 What intriguing mission can I send students on to allow them to extend their learning in a unique way?

 How can I provide my students the opportunity for an experience that will create life-long memories? (These would not be required, strictly extra-credit.)

Some of the most memorable moments my students experience do not happen in my class, and they are not required activities. For example, when studying the West and the Gold Rush, we learn about an amazing entrepreneur named Sam Brannan. After hearing about the unbelievable way he became rich without ever mining for gold, I put forth a challenge. Sam Brannan is buried in San Diego—bring me a picture of you with his gravestone. I have had literally hundreds of students over the years search through the Mt. Hope Cemetery and return with pictures. I like to give them activities that seem like missions, and they enjoy getting together with friends and tackling the challenges.

The granddaddy of all my extra-credit challenges is the March to the Sea. As part of a lesson on the impact of the automobile and how it has transformed our sense of space and time, I ask students to estimate how long it would take to get from my room to the beach. After they guess anywhere from twenty to forty minutes, I inform them that I mean by foot. They have no idea so I say that I challenge them to test it and find out. They have to touch my door and then put their hand in the ocean. It takes them about seven to ten hours! They, all on their own I might add, form into teams and show up on various Saturdays and Sundays throughout the second semester and head off as early as five in the morning. They often come up with names for their groups and even design t-shirts or wear matching clothes. The Bull Moose Party, The Tribe, The Neon Turtles, and Team Song are examples of their creativity at work. This is absolutely amazing if you think about it. Many students, including some who don't even want to come to school on a regular day, show up on a Saturday at five in the morning to walk for eight hours. Part of the magic created by the "safe-zone" of my class is the sense of camaraderie that forms among students. Over time, they get excited about conquering an insurmountable challenge with a team. The explorers collect souvenirs along the way and bring them back to my class the next week. They sound like old war buddies reminiscing about their adventures. It's an experience they will never forget.

Students will do amazing things if you can design a class and environment that is positive and empowering. Rising up to and overcoming challenges, building lifetime relationships, and forging positive connections to school won't directly result in better test scores. It will result in better people. Isn't that what we're really trying to accomplish?

THIS ISN'T FANTASY FOOTBALL

Most of my friends play fantasy football. I've always resisted their peer pressure and refused to join in. Nothing against it...just don't want to spend the time. This year, however, one of the dads started a kid's league in the neighborhood and my son joined. I watched the first games of the season with my son and his friend as they followed their players; it definitely changes how you see the game. My son's friend, Robby, is a huge Chargers fan and I watched in disbelief as he cheered after an incomplete pass from Phillip Rivers to Vincent Jackson. We were losing the game and it would have been a touchdown for our team but Jackson and Rivers were on his opponent's fantasy team. He was actually rooting against his beloved Chargers because the stats of individual players had become more important than the game.

In fantasy football, a player's worth is solely based on their individual statistics. Much of what makes a player great, and helps a team win, doesn't show up on the stat sheet. The block that set up the winning touchdown? Forget about it. It wasn't my guy who scored. Mindlessly and obsessively tracking stats can lead to a shallow view of the game.

As a basketball coach, I love to watch the player who rotates to provide defensive help, sets the proper angled screen to free up the three-point shooter, and blocks out the other team's leading rebounder. Unfortunately, the majority of fans watching the game (and everybody reading the box score in the paper) miss these crucial elements in the win. Statistics just can't properly measure the impact a player has on the game.

The exact same principle holds true when we turn school into a twisted version of fantasy sports and over-emphasize standardized testing. An intense focus on test scores can lead to a shallow and narrow view of what is important. I refuse to boil down the educational, growth, and development of my students into a statistic. Much of what is truly significant in the long run just doesn't show on the "stat sheet" provided by test scores. For example, I would much rather my kids leave my class with the strength of character and courage to fight racism when they find it, than have memorized some facts about the Civil Rights Act of 1964. I'm not saying you can't have both, I'm just pointing out that only one of those things will be measured on the test—and it *isn't* the most important one.

Why have so many schools reduced the time and emphasis they place on art, music, and physical education? The answer is beyond simple: those areas aren't measured on the all-important tests. You know where those areas are measured… in *life!* Art, music, and a healthy lifestyle help us develop a richer, deeper, and more balanced perspective. Never before have we needed more of an emphasis on the development of creativity, but schools have gone the exact opposite direction in an effort to make the best test-taking automatons possible. Our economy no longer rewards people for blindly following rules and becoming a cog in the machine. We need risk-takers, outside-the-box thinkers, and entrepreneurs; our school systems do the next generation of leaders a disservice by discouraging these very skills and attitudes. Instead of helping and encouraging them to find and develop their unique strengths, they're told to shut up, sit down, put the cell phone away, memorize these facts and fill in the bubbles.

This isn't fantasy football! Education shouldn't be about raising statistics. It *should* be about raising and fulfilling human potential. Focusing on the stats leads to a lost perspective of what is truly important—the game.

Oh, and by the way, in the game I'm talking about we are all on the same team.

BUILDING
A BETTER
PIRATE

THE AWKWARD
QUESTION

"Life is too short to be small."

BENJAMIN DISRAELI

*"Do you want to be safe and good, or do you
want to take a chance and be great?"*

JIMMY JOHNSON

Do you want to be great?

When I ask this question in my workshops, it is most often met with awkward silence, nervous shifting in the seats, and avoidance of eye contact.

Why is it such an uncomfortable question for teachers to answer? We admire athletes who want to be great. In fact, we get annoyed and disappointed with athletes who don't have the drive to fulfill their potential. Yet, it is so hard for most teachers to admit aloud that they want to be great.

Could it be that wanting to be great seems egotistical or selfish? Let's destroy that idea right away. First of all, your greatness in the classroom doesn't negatively impact or inhibit anyone else's opportunity to be great. This isn't a zero sum game. The pie is infinitely huge. In fact, your greatness only enhances the opportunities and possibilities for others. By being great, you are raising the bar and providing a model for others to emulate. Being your best possible self contributes to the school culture necessary to create the environment for greatness to flourish. In addition, your greatness with your students trickles down to all teachers who will have contact with these same kids in other classes and other years. They will leave your class a more well-rounded, self-confident, competent, and positive person. In our profession, the old saying is true: "A rising tide lifts all ships."

Being truly great requires a significant amount of extra time and effort. It demands a relentless pursuit of excellence, self-improvement, and a never-ending commitment to grow and stay on the cutting edge.

After you put in all of that extra time and effort, how much more will you see in your paycheck because of it?

Zero! That's right. Not one cent more!

So, who then benefits from your greatness?

Your students, your school, and your community all benefit. Ultimately, the *world* becomes a better place because of your greatness. Therefore, in our profession, striving for greatness is the ultimate act of unselfishness! We are in a service profession, and there is nothing egotistical or selfish about wanting to provide world-class service to our clients.

I think another reason people feel uncomfortable saying they want to be great is the group dynamic. I'm sure a certain portion of my audiences want to say "yes" to the greatness question. Unfortunately, the snide comments and eye rolling of their peers keeps them from admitting what they really want. People who are comfortable and accustomed to traveling with the pack, always riding in the middle of the peloton, often resent those trying to escape in search of something more. After all, riding in the peloton saves up to forty percent of your energy due to less wind resistance. Breaking away, on the other hand, requires a huge burst of energy and enough strength to avoid getting dragged back to the pack. Believe me, plenty of people will try to drag you back. That's why you must have a goal worth fighting for.

MEDIOCRITY DOESN'T MOTIVATE

To ascend to the level of greatness, you have to be on fire with passion and enthusiasm. Mediocrity is incapable of motivating. You just can't be on fire about mediocrity. There's no energy, no juice, and no fuel to ignite action. How could anyone be fired up about creating a lukewarm classroom envi-

> *"Having an unusually large goal is an adrenaline infusion that provides the endurance to overcome the inevitable trials and tribulations that go along with any goal."*
> TIMOTHY FERRISS

ronment where kids punch the clock, mostly behave, and then file out the door to the next class? Teaching is a tough job filled with unbelievable hardships, hurdles, and headaches. Our profession has a notoriously high burnout rate. Unless you find something big to care about, you won't make it.

Seeking greatness, on the other hand, is a journey that can ignite, stoke, and continuously fuel a raging inferno. That journey begins the instant a teacher chooses to shift his or her mindset and says, "Yes! I want to be great!"

While far from being egotistical or selfish, seeking greatness does indeed have personal benefits beyond the humanitarian ones. The decision to pursue excellence—as a teacher and as an individual—transforms teaching into an amazingly fulfilling and rewarding profession. Suddenly, it's easy to get out of the bed in the morning because you are motivated by a mighty purpose. And at the end of a long, full day, you go home feeling more energized than when you started. I know this to be true, because I see teachers, not only at my school, but all over the nation who love their jobs because they are committed to be great.

Among the general public, there is a misconception that education is completely broken and teaching has become a lost art. They harken back to some nonexistent perfect time when "things were different." Those who hold to this opinion are wrong! They don't see the same teachers I see—teachers who are unbelievably innovative and doing stunningly fantastic things in the classroom. We don't want to go back to the overly institutionalized industrial-style education of the past. That outdated, damaging, "don't smile until Christmas" mentality can and should vanish forever. We're skyrocketing forward into an educational landscape that is changing every day. In these exciting times, we must be ready to take on the challenge of redefining greatness for a whole new generation of teachers and students.

THE MIGHTY PURPOSE

"Keep away from people who belittle your ambitions. Small people always do that, but the really great make you feel that you, too, can become great."

MARK TWAIN

The media propaganda against education and teachers has reached a fever pitch of ridiculousness. It doesn't faze me one single bit. It rolls off me like water off a duck's back. I rarely engage in a debate and, when I do, I never get confrontational or lose my temper.

Why? It's simple. My purpose is too mighty to be dragged down by negativity. I just can't afford it. What I'm trying to accomplish is too significant and game changing to allow anything to slow me down.

When you have a high enough calling, it is much easier to commit yourself to doing whatever it takes to accomplish your life's purpose. You have to decide if what you're doing is worth your complete effort and full attention. If it is, don't let anything stop you. The word "decide" has an interesting etymology. It means, literally, to cut off. When you truly decide, truly commit, you are cutting off all other options. Making a decision about your life's purpose isn't something to be done lightly.

I love what George Bernard Shaw said in *Man and Superman*:

> "This is the true joy in life: the being used for a purpose recognized by yourself as a mighty one; the being thoroughly worn out before you are thrown on the scrap heap; the being a force of nature instead of a feverish, selfish little clod of ailments and grievances complaining that the world will not devote itself to making you happy."

Note that he didn't say joy results when your purpose is recognized as mighty by political pundits, radio talk-show hosts, and outsiders. He said it had to be recognized by *yourself*. Stop looking for external validation. Sure it would be nice for society at large to put the proper value on what we do, but notoriety isn't necessary for greatness or fulfillment. We know teachers today are doing more with less than at any other time in recent history. Our profession isn't broken. In the circles I frequent, there is more energy for propelling the profession forward than I can ever remember.

I can think of no higher purpose or calling than teacher. We help shape the minds of future generations. We have the ability to literally change the world. How then can anyone possibly hope to measure the extent of our greatness? With more statistics, right?

Not really, but that's exactly what current teacher evaluation models rely on to quantify teacher effectiveness. Such methods are hopelessly flawed. You can't measure a teacher's impact through standardized test scores or D/F rates. A teacher's impact can only be measured through *generations*! I like the coach who, during an end-of-season interview was asked if he thought his season was successful. He paused a moment and replied, "I won't know for another twenty years." That's it! We aren't just teaching facts to memorize or skills to learn; we're uplifting lives and helping students fulfill their human potential. We're shaping the mothers, fathers, world leaders, entrepreneurs, and artists of tomorrow. Anyone with the most rudimentary understanding of geometric progression realizes that our students will interact and influence millions. It's a mighty purpose, indeed.

That's why I agree with Shaw's comment about wanting to be thoroughly worn out by the time this life is over. I don't have time to be tired. When you're doing great work, you have a moral imperative to become the force of nature Shaw refers to. I don't want to play small—I want to be *larger than life*. Teaching is a poker game that must be played "all in." Don't allow anything to stop you. Be willing to have, as Malcolm X would say, a "by any means necessary" attitude. Don't hang around negative people; they will sap your super powers as sure as kryptonite. If people could only see what we do, they would realize we are modern day superheroes wearing the Clark Kent disguise of teacher.

Do you want to be great? Absolutely! Our purpose is too mighty for anything less.

PLAY YOUR DRUM

Little Drummer Boy has been my favorite Christmas Carol for as long as I can remember. Of all of the holiday songs, I can honestly say it is the only one that truly moves me. The idea of a young boy, too poor to afford a fitting gift for the "newborn king," attempting to honor him with what he does is a great lesson for all of us. We spend too much time stressing out and concerning ourselves with what is absent in our lives, and not enough time focusing on what really matters.

The drummer boy may not be able to afford expensive and fancy gifts, but he has something better; he can offer the gift of his unique strengths and talents. He has no material gift to offer, but what he *can* do is play his drum like no one else is capable of playing it. And so he does. The fact that his play is met with approval and acceptance from Mary and the animals is certainly of no surprise. After all, when one is engaged in pursuing one's passion and offering the very personal gift of doing what he does best, the power is undeniable and clear to all.

Isn't that what life is really all about? We all have to find our own personal "drum" and then play it the best we can. For me, I never feel more truly alive than when I'm standing in front of a class of students or a seminar room full of teachers. That's my drum I'm playing up there and I'm going to play the heck out of it. The line, "I played my best for him," is a call to arms and a challenge to meet. Forget about all of things you can't control and play *your* drum to the best of *your* abilities. Play with all the passion, enthusiasm, and heart you can muster. Nothing else really matters. You can offer no finer gift or higher honor to the world than to find out what your "drum" is and then play it for all it's worth.

WHERE DO
I START?

*"Everyone who got to where they are
had to begin where they were."*

RICHARD PAUL EVANS

"The great end of life is not knowledge but action."

THOMAS HENRY HUXLEY

Hopefully, you have found this book inspirational. At the very least, I hope you've discovered some ideas you want to apply to your teaching. Where and when should you start applying them?

Right here and right now.

"Starting" may well be one of the most difficult and under-appreciated skills of all. The world is filled with examples of people who never achieved what they wanted because they over-estimated the difficulty of

"All art is a series of recoveries from the first line. The hardest thing to do is to put down the first line. But you must."

NATHAN OLIVERA

it and never even bothered to try. You will find that taking the first step is very often the hardest part of the journey. The single most difficult part of writing my blog posts is sitting down at the computer and opening up a blank Word document. Once I've done that, half the battle is over. The hardest part of working out on a regular basis is getting to the gym or leaving the house for a walk. Working out actually makes me feel incredible, the only really difficult part is starting.

So what holds us back? What keeps us from starting? The answers to this question probably number in the thousands, if not millions. That said, the five below are the most common reasons—and they're all conquerable.

1. THE FEAR OF FAILURE

Quite simply, some people don't start what they know is in their best interest and what they really, deep down want to do, because they think their efforts will be wasted in failure.

 "Why pass up that piece of cake and go work out when I know I'm just going to quit like every other time before?"

 "I don't have the ability to learn how to use all of this new technology and, even if I do learn it, it will just change again."

 "My kids would never participate in these crazy classroom activities."

This self-defeating attitude and lack of self-confidence destroys all forward progress. You can't grow, advance, and move forward without repeatedly stumbling and falling on your face. If, as toddlers, we went into the process of learning to walk with our adult mindset, we would still be crawling. You have to be able to push through the fear and bring your work into the world.

> *"Would you like me to give you a formula for success? It's quite simple, really. Double your rate of failure."*
>
> THOMAS J. WATSON

LIFE ISN'T 100% OR FAIL

The "madness" of the 2011 NCAA basketball tournament ended with Butler University shooting the ball worse than any team I've ever seen in a championship. It was a legendarily bad game. And like any losing team, Butler received a fair amount of criticism. Honestly, all the Twitter comments about the "failure" of Butler's team made me sick. Are you kidding me? A small school comes out of nowhere to make the championship *two years* in a row, and then people piled on because the team lost both times. A low-seeded underdog making the finals two years in a row is one of the most amazing accomplishments in college basketball. But because our culture lives by the philosophy that you either win it all or you are a failure, the team was trashed. Don't buy into this B.S.! (It reminds me of when the Bills lost four Super Bowls in four years and were labeled by many as embarrassments and failures. Hello! To lose four consecutive Super Bowls, you have to *go* to four consecutive Super Bowls, which is an unbelievable accomplishment.)

As a San Diegan, I follow the SDSU Aztecs. This team had never been in the top twenty and never won an NCAA tournament game. They finished the 2011 season with thirty-four wins and three losses. They were ranked sixth in the nation, and went to the Sweet 16. Still, after losing to UConn, some claimed it was all for naught. One team wins and all

the rest are losers. What a misguided and dysfunc-
tional way to look at the world.

Do you want a guaranteed formula for disap-
pointment in life? Set up the rules of your life so that
you have to win every time or have one hundred
percent success in order to feel fulfilled.

So how does this apply to teaching? During a
recent new teacher training, a second year teacher
asked me a fantastic question. After watching me
demonstrate lots of student engagement strategies
and techniques, she asked, "When you use these
strategies do you have full engagement from one
hundred percent of your students?" I said, "OK.
I'm going to tell you the real deal. NO!! What I
have is *more* engagement than I would have had
if I didn't use these techniques." She then shared
that she feels unsuccessful when she tries to add
creative and engaging presentations because some
students still don't get into it. I think many teachers
set themselves up for failure this way by making it
a one hundred percent or nothing game. I always
strive for total engagement, but believe me, I have
behavior management problems in my class, too.
Students sneak in texts in their lap, kids stare out the
window. Striving for excellence and full engagement
is about getting better. It's about adapting, adjusting,
and trying to tweak and improve everything you do.
It's not about beating yourself up if you don't attain
some unreachable level of nirvana-like perfection.

An all or nothing mentality exacerbates the fear of failure. If you believe everything you do has to work one hundred percent of the time, you are less likely to take risks and step out of your comfort zone. I often say, "If you haven't failed in the classroom lately, you probably aren't pushing the envelope enough. You are being too safe."

I had the pleasure of working for John Wooden for three summers at his basketball camps. One of his wise sayings was that "the team that makes the most mistakes usually wins." That sounds counter-intuitive. The truth is, the team that makes the most mistakes is the team that is going for it and actually *doing* something. Playing cautiously is a recipe for failure in sports, business, teaching, love, and just about everything else. To reach the highest levels of any pursuit, you have to be willing to fall on your face.

It seems everybody is piling on teachers right now. We have become fashionable targets. Honestly, I don't let it bother me and you shouldn't either. Success isn't something that is bestowed upon you by an outside source or a test score. It doesn't come from winning the championship or going undefeated. How then can we define success? I think John Wooden said it best: "Success is peace of mind, which is a direct result of self-satisfaction in knowing you made the effort to do your best to become the best that you are capable of becoming."

He was a wise man.

2. BELIEVING YOU HAVE TO FIGURE IT ALL OUT BEFORE YOU BEGIN

Nobody has it all figured out. If I felt I had to have it all figured out before I started this book or my original seminar, I wouldn't have done either.

> *"Faith is taking the first step even when you don't see the whole staircase."*
> MARTIN LUTHER KING, JR.

To win in the classroom, you must develop the ability to take leaps of faith. The cost of having a lesson plan fail is low. Nobody is going to die if we experiment in the classroom and it doesn't work out. If my surgeon decides to experiment during my operation, that's different. If a lesson plan fails, you show up the next day and make it right. More importantly, the cost of failure is far lower than the cost of standing still and losing out on all hope for progress. Teaching is like being on a steep, smooth-sided mountain. If you stand still, not only will you fail to reach the summit, you will actually lose ground. Unless you are constantly climbing and striving to move forward, you are sliding backwards. And even though you can't see the impact you or your class will have on your students twenty years up the road, that's OK. You don't have to be able to see the top of the mountain to know that you can only get there by moving forward.

3. PERFECTIONISM

Perfectionism can paralyze. Some people don't want to act until the time is perfect and all the bugs have been worked out. Demanding perfection keeps these people from producing anything of significance because, obviously, perfection is an impossible goal. It is far more important to be prolific than it is to be perfect. I believe in adhering to the Wedding Photographer Principle. It would be outrageous for a wedding photographer to not take any pictures all day while waiting for the perfect shot. What do they do? They take hundreds of pictures from every possible angle with every possible group. Since the pictures are digital, the cost of each additional one is negligible. Then, you get the freedom and flexibility to choose your personal favorites. You are far more likely to find great pictures when there are hundreds to choose from. The same is true for your educational creations.

Kill the inner critic that blocks your creative flow. Surrender your search for the holy grail of perfection. Create freely, liberally, and in great quantities; doing so relieves any one idea of the need to be perfect.

How will you know what the best ideas are out of so many? If you can't figure it out on your own, trust me, the world will let you know. That brings up another point about relenting on your need for perfection and putting yourself out there. Unless you send your work, your art, out into the world, it doesn't count. In his book *Linchpin*, Seth Godin refers to this concept as shipping: "Shipping something out the door, doing it regularly, without hassle, emergency, or fear— this is a rare skill, something that makes you indispensable." In my inner circle of colleagues, we use this word, *ship*, to keep each other accountable. We cajole each other to continue to do the work. You can either *talk* about all of the great things you are going to do or you can actually *do* them. There is no in between. As Steve Jobs said, "Real artists ship."

What have you shipped lately?

4. LACK OF FOCUS

Time is our most precious commodity, and it is definitely a finite resource. Therefore, we just can't do it all. Too often, we fill our schedules with minutiae

> *"It's easy to say "no!" when you have a bigger "yes!" burning inside."*
>
> STEPHEN COVEY

and seem too busy to accomplish our goals. We play this trick on ourselves; it's what Steven Pressfield calls in *The War of Art,* "the resistance." Subconsciously, we know if we keep ourselves busy and over-scheduled, we won't have to face the great work we know that we should be doing. We have to do what Stephen Covey described as putting the big rocks (your priorities) in your jar of life first. The less important things can fill the extra time, just don't allow them to steal time from your priorities. Realize that any time you say yes to something, you are saying no to something else. Learn to say yes to the significant, and no to projects and activities that diminish the time and energy you need to fulfill your major purpose.

5. FEAR OF CRITICISM OR RIDICULE

> *"I can't give you a surefire formula for success, but I can give you a formula for failure: try to please everybody all the time."*
>
> HERBERT BAYARD SWOPE

You can fear it all you want…it's still coming. I'm constantly surprised how desperately we seem to crave the approval and permission of other adults and will use the lack of it to justify inaction. Criticism and ridicule come with the territory if you are going to try new ideas and be proactive rather than reactive. You'll get stuff wrong, make a fool of yourself, and many will give you grief for it.

You'll also grow, find ideas that do work, and leave the armchair quarterbacks in the dust.

DON'T LET CRITICS
STEAL YOUR SOUL

First some background, then a rant, and finally a point.

At the end of my WWII unit, I give a full lecture on the decision to use the atomic bomb on Japan. I display supporting pictures, give arguments from both sides, and show documentary footage of the aftermath of the explosion and radiation. This includes extensive survivor interviews and footage that had previously been suppressed. We discuss the moral implications of using the bomb as well as the military arguments. We ponder questions such as, "Do the ends justify the means?" "Did dropping the bomb actually save lives by immediately ending the war?" Finally, I tell them about Sadako and the "Thousand Paper Cranes." It's a story of a young girl from Hiroshima who slowly dies in the hospital from leukemia as a result of the bomb blast. She desperately tries to fold a thousand cranes so her wish to become well will be granted. The story is emotional and is a powerful moment for the class. At the end, I tell them of the monument honoring Sadako that is in the Hiroshima Peace Park and the inscription that reads, "This our cry, this our prayer, peace in the world." I bring out a garland made entirely of a thousand small cranes and then tell the class that, to honor Sadako and innocent victims of war, I will teach them to fold a paper crane. The last section of the Sadako day is spent with me leading them through the folds. Every student leaves with a self-made crane.

OK, there's the background...now comes the rant!

We just had a WASC (Western Association of Schools and Colleges) accreditation visit at our school. The visiting team was well led and left with a positive impression of our school. All things considered, it was a meaningful and productive process. But, and this is a big but, one thing happened that got my blood boiling and it has taken a long time to let it go. One of the visiting committee members came into my class during the last ten minutes of the Sadako lesson as I was leading the class through the final folds. He approached a student sitting on the counter (yes, we have more students than seats!) and asked what class it was. Upon hearing that it was U.S. History, he looked around and said judgmentally under his breath (but loud enough for multiple students in the area to hear), "What does this have to do with U.S. History?" He then walked to the back wall and left after a couple of minutes.

"What does this have to do with U.S. History?" Are you kidding me? This guy comes into my class for three minutes and sees something totally removed from any context and then drops that line? Let's forget about how unprofessional it is to say something like that in front of a group of my students. I can get over that because they all thought he was a complete idiot. They knew exactly what it had to do with U.S. History. If he really wanted to know, he could have asked me instead of making a misguided, arrogant judgment and leaving just as ignorant as he entered.

Later I learned that in one of the final leadership meetings, an English teacher was criticized because students were drawing a picture of a Greek god as part of a project on mythology. The comment was, "Is that really an example of rigor in an English class?"

Yeah, God forbid that we incorporate artistic elements and creativity into a class outside of the art department. Next thing you know, kids might start enjoying school and become well-rounded individuals.

I know I'm going to get into trouble with some of you now, but let's be careful with this word "rigor." Here's how Merriam-Webster Online Dictionary defines the word:

- "harsh inflexibility in opinion, temper, or judgment
- severity
- the quality of being unyielding or inflexible
- strictness, severity of life, austerity
- an act or instance of strictness, severity, or cruelty
- a tremor caused by a chill
- a condition that makes life difficult, challenging, or uncomfortable"

Wow! I don't want any of these definitions to describe my class. The only good thing in the whole definition is the word "challenging." Harsh inflexibility in opinion? Severity? Cruelty? A condition that makes life uncomfortable? No thanks!

I know, I know...that's not what educators mean when they throw that word around. Nevertheless, I think it's important that we clearly and carefully define what we mean by "rigor." I hope it doesn't just mean a bigger workload for students. It had better not mean more hours of homework or classes that are just harder to pass. If, instead, rigor means improving higher-order thinking skills and offering students the opportunity for meaningful and challenging work then I'm all for it. More real-world applications? Sounds good!

A lot of people who use that word have never bothered to look it up. I also think that some people have no idea what meaningful and challenging work is. After all, creativity is one of the highest forms of thinking, but some educational "reformers" don't want students to have an opportunity to express it. They see it as a "soft" skill, not "rigorous" enough. We clearly have some work to do.

Now let's move on to the point of this story. You will be criticized! In fact, the more you step outside the box and reject the culture of conformity, the more of a target you will become. When criticism comes, take a moment to evaluate it. Is the criticism an opportunity for growth? If so, learn from that instruction. But realize, too, that your critic may have no idea what they are talking about! In that case, ignore it.

You have to have the intestinal fortitude, self-confidence, and personal power to press on and do what you know is right for your students. Don't allow misguided and ill-informed critics to steal your enthusiasm for innovation. If you let them, they will sap you of the strength needed to persist in this brutally tough profession. You have to learn how to take a punch, bob and weave, and keep moving forward. What you do as an educator is too important to let somebody standing on the sidelines prevent you from being the absolutely most powerful teacher you can be. Some people will just never get it! That's OK, that's their problem; you can't let it become yours.

I don't think anyone has ever said it better than Teddy Roosevelt:

> "It is not the critic who counts; not the man who points out how the strong man stumbles, or where the doer of deeds could have done them better. The credit belongs to the man who is actually in the arena, whose face is marred by dust and sweat and blood; who strives valiantly; who errs, who comes short again and again, because there is no effort without error and shortcoming; but who does actually strive to do the deeds; who knows great enthusiasms, the great devotions; who spends himself in a worthy cause; who at the best knows in the end the triumph of high achievement, and who at the worst, if he fails, at least fails while daring greatly, so that his place shall never be with those cold and timid souls who neither know victory nor defeat."

It's easy to stand against the back wall and be a critic. Meanwhile, the rest of us will keep wiping the dust, sweat, and blood off our face because we're in the arena.

WHEN IN DOUBT, TAKE ACTION

"Thinking will not overcome fear but action will."

W. CLEMENT STONE

The best way to overcome fear is to take action. The more action you take and the quicker you take it, the better.

The best way to solidify your commitment to achieving your goals is also to take action. The best way to overcome the obstacles on your path to greatness is build up enough momentum through action that you can roll right over them.

The Law of Inertia states that an object at rest will stay at rest unless a force acts on it and that an object in motion will stay in motion unless a force acts on it. To overcome inertia and start moving forward, we must exert great force. Once we are in motion we are more likely to stay in motion. This is especially true if we build up speed and momentum. If you have to stop a car from rolling down the street, would you rather it be rolling at two miles per hour or sixty miles per hour? If it's rolling sixty miles per hour it will roll right over the top of you and keep going. We want to be rolling sixty miles per hour towards our goals so that obstacles in our path get steamrolled and are distant memories in the rearview mirror. The reason

"Action is the foundational key to all success."

PABLO PICASSO

many people get held up by problems and obstacles is that they haven't built up enough momentum. Take your foot off of the brake and step on the gas!

I have seen people take twenty minutes to get into a pool. First one foot, then the other, standing around complaining that it's too cold. Gradually, they move a little deeper. I have also seen people

"*Whatever you can do or dream you can, begin it. Boldness has genius, power and magic in it.*"

JOHANN WOLFGANG VON GOETHE

walk right over to the pool and jump in. Fear, analysis paralysis, and lack of confidence can make what should be a simple and quick turn into a torturous and drawn out process. Just rip off the bandage, suck it up, and move forward with consistent and massive action.

FINDING A CREW

"I not only use all the brains that I have,
but all the brains that I can borrow."

WOODROW WILSON

ll pirates travel with a crew; you can't sail, navigate, and fight battles all on your own. One of the most rewarding parts of teaching is the personal and professional relationships we develop on our voyage. I am the teacher I am today because of the relationships I have developed. Having a diverse crew is in your best interest. Don't be limited by your subject, grade level, school, or even profession. Take counsel from a wide variety of people and seek out multiple perspectives.

Look for opportunities to hone your craft and find educators willing and open to engage in meaningful conversations about "the work." Read widely about education and related fields and attend conferences whenever possible. I always leave conferences feeling energized by both the new ideas I hear and by being in the same physical space with others who are dedicated to improving themselves. You might make a connection that will last a lifetime.

The power of social media means no teacher need feel isolated. For example, I am part of a huge group of educators who regularly connect on Twitter. I have daily access to incredible professional development resources by tapping into my Professional Learning Network (PLN). I participate in multiple educational chats on Twitter, including #sschat, which is comprised of a fantastic group of social studies teachers from literally all over the world. No matter what you teach or at what level, you'll find great teachers and administrators talking about it on Twitter. Feel free to connect with me at @burgessdave if you need help getting started.

COLLABORATION VS. KILLABORATION

I strongly believe in the power of collaboration, but I don't believe the final goal of such work should be to come to a single "right" way of teaching. Collaboration can make all contributors better teachers as they are exposed to others' ideas and have a chance to draw on the collective intelligence of the group. Collaborative environments can challenge your thinking and push you to places you might not have reached without the support of your peers. However, I have also seen collaboration used to force conformity and stifle creativity. It's a fine line.

I like to think of collaboration as a type of mastermind group, as described by Napoleon Hill in his classic book *Think and Grow Rich*. Hill defines a mastermind group as, "Coordination of knowledge and effort, in a spirit of harmony, between two or more people, for the attainment of a definite purpose." He further says that, "When a group of individual brains are coordinated and function in a spirit of Harmony, the increased energy created through that alliance, becomes available to every individual brain in the group." He doesn't say that every individual will start thinking alike or come to any one single answer, but rather that each individual will be able to function at a higher level through their harmonious participation. In contrast, if the way collaboration is set up, driven, and monitored on your campus does not contribute to it being accomplished "in a spirit of harmony," it will not be effective.

Wonderfully creative, innovative, and practical results can come out of the collaborative process. Therefore, increasing communication, thoughtful conversation, and opportunities for educators to interact and collaborate should be a major goal on your campus. Let's just be sure that the "definite purpose" of collaboration is improving education, not simply standardizing it.

Be wary of people selling complete programs that will supposedly solve all educational problems. I believe that there is no single answer for how to fix our schools but that we should take the best ideas from everything that we can find.

CLASSROOM KUNG FU

Bruce Lee is probably the most famous name in martial arts history, but most people know little about him other than what they have garnered from watching his movies or hearing about his untimely death. Lee was a true visionary who transformed the martial arts landscape with his revolutionary style of teaching; I believe we can learn a lot from this master.

Lee was trained in the classic Wing Chun style of kung fu, but in 1967, he broke away from it and created his own philosophy which he called Jeet Kune Do. He felt that martial artists were artificially restricting their options by blind adherence to a particular style. Lee believed the most effective and practical plan would incorporate the best elements from multiple styles. He railed against the endless repetition of beautiful and flowery forms completely outside of the context of how those moves work in the real world. He was unconcerned with how "pretty" a move was; he only cared that it was effective in the real world. An actual combat situation is messy and unpredictable. As we know, classrooms are the same way. Great teaching gets messy sometimes and we have to constantly be aware of the changing landscape in our rooms and make "moves" based on what works, not on what is necessarily theoretically ideal or, God forbid, scripted. Great teaching, like a fight, can't be scripted.

Occasionally, I watch professional development sessions and get the immediate sense the presenter is great at doing the classical forms but would get their ass kicked in front of a real class. Sorry to say it, but you know I'm right. (Not to say that they have nothing of value to offer, but their real-world moves could use some work.)

Districts and schools always seem to be investing in the latest, greatest program to solve all of their problems. It doesn't work that way. No one program contains all of the best answers, just like no martial art style contains all the best moves. The best martial artist may take a throw from judo, a kick from tae kwon do, and a strike from karate. Likewise, teachers should not allow themselves to be pigeon-holed by some particular doctrine or program. Instead, we should always be seeking to add more and more effective "moves" to our teaching style—regardless of the source.

Sometimes outside forces try to lock us into a particular style. Sometimes we do it to ourselves. Confession time! For years I gloried in being the "non-tech guy" and quickly rejected opportunities to incorporate more technology saying, "Hey, it's not my style." That attitude is just like the martial artist who rejects a practical and effective move because it is not a part of Wing Chun or whatever style to which they belong. Bruce Lee was right. Sometimes labeling and declaring a style places limits on your growth. He was fearful that his followers would do this to Jeet Kune Do and constantly admonished them to not be concerned with the name.

Have you limited yourself by blindly following a style or program? Are you training students to do beautiful and perfect repetitions of classical forms completely removed from real world applications? In a real fight you don't just start doing your moves in the prescribed order you learned them. Likewise, we don't want students who can just spit out facts, formulas, and equations. We want students who can take what they have learned and intelligently apply it to the real world around them.

Stay fluid, keep learning, and keep up the relentless search for what is most effective. Feel free to leave some of your classical training behind. Teachers and students could both benefit from adopting a Jeet Kune Do philosophy in the classroom.

FINDING
TREASURE

*"Once you've done the mental work, there comes
a point you have to throw yourself into the
action and put your heart on the line."*

PHIL JACKSON

I feel completely blessed that you have chosen to take this journey with me. As I have traveled to conferences, keynotes, convocations, and campuses, I have been overwhelmed by the passion, enthusiasm, and kind receptions I have received from educators. Ours is an absolutely amazing profession filled with talented people who make me proud to call myself a teacher.

If this book has inspired you, encouraged you, or helped you find some educational treasure, I would love for you to share that with me. Hearing your thoughts and experiences with trying these ideas in your classroom helps to make this all worthwhile. You can contact me any time at **outrageousteaching@gmail.com** and please feel free to sign up for my free email list at **http://daveburgess.com**. Signing up also gives you access to the featured content link on my site that includes extra resources, PDFs and videos.

Thank you for helping to spread the word about the *Teach Like a PIRATE* book and philosophy. I hope to cross paths with you as we explore uncharted territories and brave new adventures.

Thank you,
Dave Burgess

ABOUT THE AUTHOR

DAVE BURGESS is the *New York Times* best-selling author of *Teach Like a PIRATE* and co-author of *P is for PIRATE: Inspirational ABC's for Educators.* He received national recognition as recipient of the 2014 BAMMY Award for Secondary School Teacher of the Year presented by the Academy of Education Arts and Sciences.

As an award-winning teacher from San Diego, California, he was recognized as Teacher of the Year, a Golden Apple recipient, and a faculty standout for 17 consecutive years in categories such as Most Entertaining, Most Energetic, and Most Dramatic. He specializes in teaching hard-to-reach, hard-to-motivate students with techniques that incorporate showmanship and creativity. His dynamic and inspirational message coupled with his outrageously energetic performance style has transformed classrooms and sparked an educational revolution around the world.

MORE FROM

DAVE BURGESS
Consulting, Inc.

P is for PIRATE
Inspirational ABC's for Educators
By Dave and Shelley Burgess (@Burgess_Shelley)

Teaching is an adventure that stretches the imagination and calls for creativity every day! In *P is for Pirate*, husband and wife team, Dave and Shelley Burgess, encourage and inspire educators to make their classrooms fun and exciting places to learn. Tapping into years of personal experience and drawing on the insights of more than seventy educators, the authors offer a wealth of ideas for making learning and teaching more fulfilling than ever before.

The Innovator's Mindset
Empower Learning, Unleash Talent, and Lead a Culture of Creativity
By George Couros (@gcouros)

The traditional system of education requires students to hold their questions and compliantly stick to the scheduled curriculum. But our job as educators is to provide new and better opportunities for our students. It's time to recognize that compliance doesn't foster innovation, encourage critical thinking, or inspire creativity—and those are the skills our students need to succeed. In *The Innovator's Mindset*, George Couros encourages teachers and administrators to empower their learners to wonder, to explore—and to become forward-thinking leaders.

Pure Genius
Building a Culture of Innovation and Taking 20%
Time to the Next Level
By Don Wettrick (@DonWettrick)

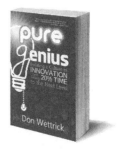

For far too long, schools have been bastions of boredom, killers of creativity, and way too comfortable with compliance and conformity. In *Pure Genius*, Don Wettrick explains how collaboration—with experts, students, and other educators—can help you create interesting, and even life-changing, opportunities for learning. Wettrick's book inspires and equips educators with a systematic blueprint for teaching innovation in any school.

Learn Like a PIRATE
Empower Your Students to Collaborate, Lead, and
Succeed
By Paul Solarz (@PaulSolarz)

Today's job market demands that students be prepared to take responsibility for their lives and careers. We do them a disservice if we teach them how to earn passing grades without equipping them to take charge of their education. In *Learn Like a PIRATE*, Paul Solarz explains how to design classroom experiences that encourage students to take risks and explore their passions in a stimulating, motivating, and supportive environment where improvement, rather than grades, is the focus. Discover how student-led classrooms help students thrive and develop into self-directed, confident citizens who are capable of making smart, responsible decisions, all on their own.

Ditch That Textbook
Free Your Teaching and Revolutionize Your Classroom
By Matt Miller (@jmattmiller)

Textbooks are symbols of centuries-old education. They're often outdated as soon as they hit students' desks. Acting "by the textbook" implies compliance and a lack of creativity. It's time to ditch those textbooks—and those textbook assumptions about learning! In *Ditch That Textbook*, teacher and blogger Matt Miller encourages educators to throw out meaningless, pedestrian teaching and learning practices. He empowers them to evolve and improve on old, standard, teaching methods. *Ditch That Textbook* is a support system, toolbox, and manifesto to help educators free their teaching and revolutionize their classrooms.

50 Things You Can Do with Google Classroom
By Alice Keeler and Libbi Miller (@alicekeeler, @MillerLibbi)

It can be challenging to add new technology to the classroom but it's a must if students are going to be well-equipped for the future. Alice Keeler and Libbi Miller shorten the learning curve by providing a thorough overview of the Google Classroom App. Part of Google Apps for Education (GAfE), Google Classroom was specifically designed to help teachers save time by streamlining the process of going digital. Complete with screenshots, *50 Things You Can Do with Google Classroom* provides ideas and step-by-step instructions to help teachers implement this powerful tool.

50 Things to Go Further with Google Classroom
A Student-Centered Approach
By Alice Keeler and Libbi Miller (@alicekeeler, @MillerLibbi)

Today's technology empowers educators to move away from the traditional classroom where teachers lead and students work independently—each doing the same thing. In *50 Things to Go Further with Google Classroom: A Student-Centered Approach*, authors and educators Alice Keeler and Libbi Miller offer inspiration and resources to help you create a digitally rich, engaging, student-centered environment. They show you how to tap into the power of individualized learning that is possible with Google Classroom.

140 Twitter Tips for Educators
Get Connected, Grow Your Professional Learning Network, and Reinvigorate Your Career
By Brad Currie, Billy Krakower, and Scott Rocco (@bradmcurrie,
@wkrakower, @ScottRRocco)

Whatever questions you have about education or about how you can be even better at your job, you'll find ideas, resources, and a vibrant network of professionals ready to help you on Twitter. In *140 Twitter Tips for Educators*, #Satchat hosts and founders of Evolving Educators, Brad Currie, Billy Krakower, and Scott Rocco offer step-by-step instructions to help you master the basics of Twitter, build an online following, and become a Twitter rock star.

Master the Media

How Teaching Media Literacy Can Save Our
Plugged-in World
By Julie Smith (@julnilsmith)

Written to help teachers and parents educate
the next generation, *Master the Media* explains the
history, purpose, and messages behind the media.
The point isn't to get kids to unplug; it's to help
them make informed choices, understand the difference between truth and
lies, and discern perception from reality. Critical thinking leads to smarter
decisions—and it's why media literacy can save the world.

The Zen Teacher

Creating Focus, Simplicity, and Tranquility in the
Classroom
By Dan Tricarico (@thezenteacher)

Teachers have incredible power to influence—
even improve—the future. In *The Zen Teacher*,
educator, blogger, and speaker Dan Tricarico provides practical, easy-to-use techniques to help
teachers be their best—unrushed and fully focused—so they can maximize
their performance and improve their quality of life. In this introductory
guide, Dan Tricarico explains what it means to develop a Zen practice—
something that has nothing to do with religion and everything to do with
your ability to thrive in the classroom.

eXPlore Like a Pirate
Gamification and Game-Inspired Course Design to
Engage, Enrich, and Elevate Your Learners
By Michael Matera (@MrMatera)

Are you ready to transform your classroom into an experiential world that flourishes on collaboration and creativity? Then set sail with classroom game designer and educator Michael Matera as he reveals the possibilities and power of game-based learning. In *eXPlore Like a Pirate*, Matera serves as your experienced guide to help you apply the most motivational techniques of gameplay to your classroom. You'll learn gamification strategies that will work with and enhance (rather than replace) your current curriculum and discover how these engaging methods can be applied to any grade level or subject.

Your School Rocks ... So Tell People!
Passionately Pitch and Promote the Positives
Happening on Your Campus
By Ryan McLane and Eric Lowe (@McLane_Ryan, @EricLowe21)

Great things are happening in your school every day. The problem is, no one beyond your school walls knows about them. School principals Ryan McLane and Eric Lowe want to help you get the word out! In *Your School Rocks ... So Tell People!* McLane and Lowe offer more than seventy immediately actionable tips along with easy-to-follow instructions and links to video tutorials. This practical guide will equip you to create an effective and manageable communication strategy using social media tools. Learn how to keep your students' families and community connected, informed, and excited about what's going on in your school.

Play Like a Pirate
Engage Students with Toys, Games, and Comics
By Quinn Rollins (@jedikermit)

Yes! Serious learning can be seriously fun. In *Play Like a Pirate*, Quinn Rollins offers practical, engaging strategies and resources that make it easy to integrate fun into your curriculum. Regardless of the grade level you teach, you'll find inspiration and ideas that will help you engage your students in unforgettable ways.

The Classroom Chef
Sharpen your lessons. Season your classes. Make math meaningful.
By John Stevens and Matt Vaudrey (@Jstevens009, @MrVaudrey)

In *The Classroom Chef*, math teachers and instructional coaches John Stevens and Matt Vaudrey share their secret recipes, ingredients, and tips for serving up lessons that engage students and help them "get" math. You can use these ideas and methods as-is, or better yet, tweak them and create your own enticing educational meals. The message the authors share is that, with imagination and preparation, every teacher can be a Classroom Chef.

How Much Water Do We Have?
5 Success Principles for Conquering Any Challenge and Thriving in Times of Change
By Pete Nunweiler with Kris Nunweiler

In *How Much Water Do We Have?* Pete Nunweiler identifies five key elements—information, planning, motivation, support, and leadership—that are necessary for the success of any goal, life transition, or challenge. If you're feeling stressed out, overwhelmed, or uncertain at work or at home, pause and look for the signs of dehydration. Learn how to find, acquire, and use the 5 Waters of Success—so you can share them with your team and family members.

The Writing on the Classroom Wall
How Posting Your Most Passionate Beliefs about
Education Can Empower Your Students, Propel Your
Growth, and Lead to a Lifetime of Learning
By Steve Wyborney (@SteveWyborney)

In *The Writing on the Classroom Wall*, Steve Wyborney
explains how posting and discussing Big Ideas can lead to
deeper learning. You'll learn why sharing your ideas will sharpen and refine
them. You'll also be encouraged to know that the Big Ideas you share don't
have to be profound to make a profound impact on learning. In fact, Steve
explains, it's okay if some of your ideas fall off the wall. What matters most
is sharing them.

Kids Deserve It!
Pushing Boundaries and Challenging Conventional
Thinking
By Todd Nesloney and Adam Welcome

(@TechNinjaTodd, @awelcome)

In *Kids Deserve It!*, Todd and Adam encourage you
to think big and make learning fun and meaningful for
students. Their high-tech, high-touch, and highly engaging practices will
inspire you to take risks, shake up the status quo, and be a champion for
your students. While you're at it, you just might rediscover why you became
an educator in the first place.

Instant Relevance
Using Today's Experiences to Teach Tomorrow's Lessons
By Denis Sheeran (@MathDenisNJ)

Every day, students in schools around the world ask the
question, "When am I ever going to use this in real life?"
In *Instant Relevance*, author and keynote speaker Denis
Sheeran equips you to create engaging lessons from experiences and events that matter to your students. Learn how to help your
students see meaningful connections between the real world and what they
learn in the classroom—because that's when learning sticks.

LAUNCH
Using Design Thinking to Boost Creativity and Bring Out the Maker in Every Student
By John Spencer and A.J. Juliani (@spencerideas, @ajjuliani)

Something happens in students when they define themselves as makers and inventors and creators. They discover powerful skills—problem-solving, critical thinking, and imagination—that will help them shape the world's future … our future. In *LAUNCH*, John Spencer and A.J. Juliani provide a process that can be incorporated into every class at every grade level … even if you don't consider yourself a "creative teacher." And if you dare to innovate and view creativity as an essential skill, you will empower your students to change the world—starting right now.

Escaping the School Leader's Dunk Tank
How to Prevail When Others Want to See You Drown
By Rebecca Coda and Rick Jetter (@RebeccaCoda, @RickJetter)

No school leader is immune to the effects of discrimination, bad politics, revenge, or ego-driven coworkers. These kinds of dunk-tank situations can make an educator's life miserable. By sharing real-life stories and insightful research, the authors (who are dunk-tank survivors themselves) equip school leaders with the practical knowledge and emotional tools necessary to survive and, better yet, avoid getting "dunked."

Start. Right. Now.
Teach and Lead for Excellence
By Todd Whitaker, Jeff Zoul, and Jimmy Casas (@ToddWhitaker, @Jeff_Zoul, @casas_jimmy)

In their work leading up to *Start. Right. Now.* Todd Whitaker, Jeff Zoul, and Jimmy Casas studied educators from across the nation and discovered four key behaviors of excellence: Excellent leaders and teachers Know the Way, Show the Way, Go the Way, and Grow Each Day. If you are ready to take the first step toward excellence, this motivating book will put you on the right path.

Lead Like a PIRATE

Make School Amazing for Your Students and Staff
By Shelley Burgess and Beth Houf (@Burgess_Shelley, @BethHouf)

In *Lead Like a PIRATE*, education leaders Shelley Burgess and Beth Houf map out the character traits necessary to captain a school or district. You'll learn where to find the treasure that's already in your classrooms and schools—and how to bring out the very best in your educators. This book will equip and encourage you to be relentless in your quest to make school amazing for your students, staff, parents, and communities.

Teaching Math with Google Apps

50 G Suite Activities
By Alice Keeler and Diana Herrington (@AliceKeeler, @mathdiana)

Google Apps give teachers the opportunity to interact with students in a more meaningful way than ever before, while G Suite empowers students to be creative, critical thinkers who collaborate as they explore and learn. In *Teaching Math with Google Apps*, educators Alice Keeler and Diana Herrington demonstrate fifty different ways to bring math classes into to the twenty-first century with easy-to-use technology.

Table Talk Math

A Practical Guide for Bringing Math into Everyday Conversations
By John Stevens (@Jstevens009)

Making math part of families' everyday conversations is a powerful way to help children and teens learn to love math. In *Table Talk Math*, John Stevens offers parents (and teachers!) ideas for initiating authentic, math-based conversations that will get kids notice and be curious about all the numbers, patterns, and equations in the world around them.

Shift This!
How to Implement Gradual Change for Massive Impact in Your Classroom
By Joy Kirr (@JoyKirr)

Establishing a student-led culture that isn't focused on grades and homework but on individual responsibility and personalized learning may seem like a daunting task—especially if you think you have to do it all at once. But significant change is possible, sustainable, and even easy when it happens little by little. In *Shift This!*, educator and speaker Joy Kirr explains how to make gradual shifts—in your thinking, teaching, and approach to classroom design—that will have a massive impact in your classroom. Make the first shift today!

Unmapped Potential
An Educator's Guide to Lasting Change
By Julie Hasson and Missy Lennard (@PPrincipals)

No matter where you are in your educational career, chances are you have, at times, felt overwhelmed and overworked. Maybe you feel that way right now. If so, you aren't alone. But the more important news is that things can get better! You simply need the right map to guide you from frustrated to fulfilled. *Unmapped Potential* offers advice and practical strategies to help you find your unique path to becoming the kind of educator—the kind of person—you want to be.

Shattering the Perfect Teacher Myth
6 Truths That Will Help You THRIVE as an Educator
By Aaron Hogan (@aaron_hogan)

The idyllic myth of the perfect teacher perpetuates unrealistic expectations that erode self-confidence and set teachers up for failure. Author and educator Aaron Hogan is on a mission to shatter the myth of the perfect teacher by equipping educators with strategies that help them shift out of survival mode and THRIVE.

Social LEADia
Moving Students from Digital Citizenship to Digital Leadership
By Jennifer Casa-Todd (@JCasaTodd)

Equipping students for their future begins by helping them become digital leaders now. In our networked society, students need to learn how to leverage social media to connect to people, passions, and opportunities to grow and make a difference. *Social LEADia* offers insight and engaging stories to help you shift the focus at school and at home from digital citizenship to digital leadership.

Spark Learning
3 Keys to Embracing the Power of Student Curiosity
By Ramsey Musallam (@ramusallam)

Inspired by his popular TED Talk "3 Rules to Spark Learning," this book combines brain science research, proven teaching methods, and Ramsey's personal story to empower you to improve your students' learning experiences by inspiring inquiry and harnessing its benefits. If you want to engage students in more interesting and effective learning, this is the book for you.

Ditch That Homework
Practical Strategies to Help Make Homework Obsolete
By Matt Miller and Alice Keeler (@jmattmiller, @alicekeeler)

In *Ditch That Homework*, Matt Miller and Alice Keeler discuss the pros and cons of homework, why teachers assign it, and what life could look like without it. As they evaluate the research and share parent and teacher insights, the authors offer a convincing case for ditching homework and replacing it with more effective and personalized learning methods.

The Four O'Clock Faculty
A Rogue Guide to Revolutionizing Professional Development
By Rich Czyz (@RACzyz)

Author Rich Czyz is on a mission to revolutionize professional learning for all educators. In *The Four O'Clock Faculty*, Rich identifies ways to make PD meaningful, efficient, and, above all, personally relevant. This book is a practical guide that reveals why some PD is so awful and what you can do to change the model for the betterment of you and your colleagues.

Culturize
Every Student. Every Day. Whatever It Takes.
By Jimmy Casas (@casas_jimmy)

In *Culturize*, author and education leader Jimmy Casas shares insights into what it takes to cultivate a community of learners who embody the innately human traits our world desperately needs, such as kindness, honesty, and compassion. His stories reveal how these "soft skills" can be honed while meeting and exceeding academic standards of twenty-first-century learning.

Code Breaker
Increase Creativity, Remix Assessment, and Develop a Class of Coder Ninjas!
By Brian Aspinall (@mraspinall)

Code Breaker equips you to use coding in your classroom to turn curriculum expectations into skills. Students learn how to identify problems, develop solutions, and use computational thinking to apply and demonstrate their learning. Best of all, you don't have to be a "computer geek" to empower your students with these essential skills.

The Wild Card

7 Steps to an Educator's Creative Breakthrough
By Hope and Wade King (@hopekingteach, @wadeking7)

Have you ever wished you were more creative… or that your students were more engaged in your lessons? *The Wild Card* is your step-by-step guide to experiencing a creative breakthrough in your classroom with your students. Wade and Hope King show you how to draw on your authentic self to deliver your content creatively and be the wild card who changes the game for your learners.

76357812R00117

Made in the USA
San Bernardino, CA
11 May 2018